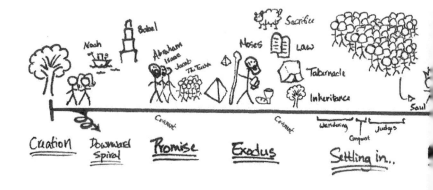

Creation   Downward   Promise   Exodus   Settling in...
            Spiral

the Bible is
beautiful

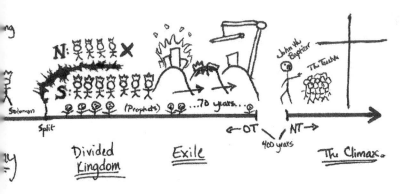

THE BIBLE IS BEAUTIFUL

BRETT DAVIS

FIRST WORDS......10

01 CREATION......22

02 DOWNWARD SPIRAL......32

03 PROMISE......46

04 THE EXODUS......60

05 ELECTED......72

06 SETTLING IN......86

07 MONARCHY......102

08 DIVIDED KINGDOM......118

09 CURSE OF EXILE......132

10 ANTICIPATION......144

11 CLIMAX PART ONE......158

12 CLIMAX PART TWO......172

13 KING OF THE UNIVERSE......192

14 THE FINAL SACRIFICE......204

15 THE TRUE EXODUS......218

16 THE NEW COVENANT......230

17 GOD WITH US......244

18 THE LAW OF LOVE......258

19 TRULY HUMAN......270

20 THE INHERITANCE......284

LAST WORDS......295

APPENDIX: CHEAT SHEET......297

INDEX: SCRIPTURAL REFERENCES......298

first words

Several months ago, I saw an online poll asking the following question: *"What time of year do you start reading Lord of the Rings?"*

Notice how the question is "when" not "if."

The question is not if people read these books every year; the question is when they do it. Their reading the books is assumed. (And it turns out that around 60-65 percent of those surveyed begin their annual reading of Tolkien's epic in the autumn.)

Think about it: every year a small portion of the world's population begins rereading a sprawling, complex, multi-layered story. A story which is rather intimidating and inaccessible at first glance, filled with all kinds of exotic names, places, languages and cultures.

And yet they return to this story year after year.

They marinate in it. They soak it up.

They relish their time there.
They reflect on it with friends.

The story is beautiful, and they love it.

What intrigues me most about Tolkien fans' annual pilgrimage through Middle Earth is how no one makes them reread the story.

No one twists their arms so they'll get away and spend some "quiet time" reading it... you couldn't keep them away.

None of them feel guilty if they get busy and cannot read for several days or weeks... they can't wait to get back to it.

Very few of them probably allow themselves to miss reading for very long... they count this as absolute joy.

It would be absurd to count how many lines, paragraphs or pages they have read for that day—that's obviously missing the point.

When they talk with other fans, it could never be stale or obligatory—they love, love, love re-living this story.

The way that Tolkien fans approach Lord of the Rings intrigues me because it reminds me of reading the Bible. Or what reading the Bible can and should be.

* * *

There are two things I would look for in an author writing a book: expertise or experience. Preferably both. And since I'm young, I'm disqualified from having very much of either. This book is purely a product of excitement.

Confession time: I remember during my first weeks of seminary sitting in Old Testament Theology and thinking, "Seminary is going to be fantastic —except for all the nitty gritty of reading the Bible."

Having grown up arrogant as a pastor's kid, I already knew all about the Bible. I wanted to move on to something more grand, something more innovative, something more relevant. But the more I began studying the "nitty gritty" of the Bible, the more I was humbled and the more excited I grew.

Humility and excitement often go together.

There's a reason the Bible is the best-selling book of all time, a reason it's been shaping communities and cultures for centuries, a reason it's been studied and revered by hundreds of millions.

The Bible, you see, tells an epic story—the Story of God. This story includes the origins of the universe and you and me and the meaning of everything. It's breath-taking when you start catching a glimpse of it.

Like Lord of the Rings (or any other epic), the Bible intimidates us at first glance. It takes us to ancient, foreign places with strangely-named people. Its story is told through different genres (narratives, poems, letters, etc) each with a different voice and each playing a particular yet vital role. It sprawls out over literally more than a thousand years with dozens of authors carrying it along. And as a diverse library of ancient documents that shouldn't gel together, it's got an almost spooky cohesion.

Perhaps most exciting, however, is how the story chases us.
The Bible relentlessly pursues its readers. It's not a neutral read.
Scripture wants something from us.
The Bible wants us to fall headlong into it.

Scripture is meant to be marinated in, soaked up and then—most essential—lived out. As we read its pages, the Bible pursues us because it wants to redefine the stories of our lives, our families, our cultures and ultimately the shape of history.

Dozens of other voices crowd us on a daily basis, competing to shape and define our lives:

Power, pleasure, success, greed, nationalism, entertainment, popularity and many others—they all tell their own stories. They sing like sirens about the ultimate meaning and shape of our lives. We're intimately acquainted with many of them and (God help us) we've begun to believe them. And we slowly start to assume they are the only options out there.

But the Bible makes a quiet claim over its hearers.
It extends a steady invitation to its readers.
It is another voice in the world. It is another option to shape us.

For thousands of years, Christians have come to the Bible as humanity's most promising guide for beginning to understand the meaning of existence. The Christian Church has claimed this because we believe that the Bible has mysteriously been inspired by God himself. This means the Creator of our universe has tied up himself with this book in an absolutely unique way. He has authored and enacted a supreme Story of history.

The following pages aim to serve as an introductory framework for reading this Story—a crash course in the Bible. I'm confident that many people (Christians included) would love to read, study and meditate on the Bible. But I'm also concerned that nobody has ever introduced them to it in a way they found compelling.

Perhaps someone worked very hard to make it seem boring.
Making the Bible boring should be criminalized.

I don't claim that this book is comprehensive in any way.

There are flagrant omissions.
Much has been simplified.

Obviously some is interpretation.

Many moments during the writing process were filled with an unexpected despair as I began realizing that writing this sort of introduction to the Bible is filled with dangers around every turn.

Because not everything *can* be said.
Much *has to be* simplified.

Scripture—as well as almost all of life—*must* be interpreted.

But driving me forward through the writing was recognition of a greater danger than all this—a greater danger than omitting, simplifying or interpreting. There is a greater danger than the danger of not saying everything:

The danger of saying nothing.

There is a terrible danger that we as Christians (forget any other type of person for the moment) will say nothing at all about the Bible. The danger that we speak little about the Bible because we know little of it. Sure, we know quite a lot about "praise music" and "good Christian morals" and "popular church trends." But what of the grand testimony of our faith?

To be sure, we occasionally crack the Bible to reinforce a few beliefs that we've been spoon-fed. But we're not exploring the Bible, wrestling with the Bible or being captivated by the Bible.

The great danger is that a generation of Christians do not know the story of the Bible—and that our lives and our churches are being shaped by other stories.

If we don't know The Story, how can we be transformed by it?

How can we retell it?
How can we live it?

Now to my point—If this book remains just another book that you read but it never pushes you into living, breathing, studying and celebrating the Bible itself, then we're all wasting our time.

This book is not the Bible, in case you were ever confused.

This book is pointing you to the Bible.

I want you to read the Bible.
I want you to love the Bible.

I want you to be transformed by God's Spirit through the Bible.

And I honestly believe that God will do this for all of us if we will only approach willingly and humbly.

There are at least two ways I would recommend reading this book. The first would be just to **read it straight through**, allowing yourself to watch the overall shape and movement of the Christian story. But then I would also *highly* recommend **reading with a Bible next to you** so you can ground yourself in the text itself. And I would recommend doing that with whatever translation of the Bible you can easily read.

The layout of this book roughly follows the flow of the Bible:

Part One traces the story of Israel that climaxes in Jesus of Nazareth—essentially spanning from Genesis to John (the entire Old Testament and the first four books of the New Testament). This part is largely chronological. The Wisdom literature (Job to Song of Songs) will be mentioned briefly, and many of the Prophets (Isaiah to Malachi) will be woven into their respective places in the story. I recommend marking up your table of contents and the pages of your Bible if that helps you. It does me.

Part Two looks back at Israel's long story through the lens of Jesus and begins asking, "What does this story mean for us now?" This part spans from Acts to Revelation (the remainder of the New Testament) and is more thematic in nature. My hope is that tracing a few prominent themes of the earliest Christian message will give you better footing as you read it.

None of us ever master the Bible and this book certainly won't make you a Bible expert. Certain tough spots will almost certainly still be confusing or overwhelming. But the following pages will be helpful in orienting yourself in God's grand and beautiful story.

You'll notice that there are plenty of footnotes throughout the course of the book.[1] The vast majority of these footnotes are references to Scripture pointing you to entire chapters and (other times) to specific verses.

---

[1] Like this one. Nothing intimidating about it.

A word of caution: many Christians use their "favorite verses" (the verses they know) as "proofs" for certain beliefs without knowing much about its place in the surrounding chapter or book, much less how it fits within the Bible as a whole. This is *not* a helpful way to read the Bible.

The footnotes are definitely not trying to promote this sort of practice. Instead the footnotes are meant to be guides for helping you steer and navigate the expansive ocean of the Bible. Think of them as "anchors" that give you starting places to jump in, explore and splash around.[2] The footnotes—and every other bit of this book—are starting points not finish lines.

* * *

So as we begin our journey through the Bible, prepare to be dazzled by its beautiful, compelling story—and transformed by the Spirit of its beautiful, crucified God.

God has told the Story of stories, and we're invited to find our stories within it. And if we will come to the pages of this story with humility, we will discover its beauty:

Elegant beauty assuring us of its divine design.
Reliable beauty training us for wise and wondrous lives.

Enduring beauty crackling with energy to upend injustice.
Powerful beauty demanding our allegiance.

Mysterious beauty answering (and silencing) our questions.
Terrifying beauty wounding as it heals.

---

[2] When I quote passages of Scripture, *I will italicize the words.* Then you can glance down at these friendly footnotes for the reference and maybe some additional thoughts.

Welcome to the Bible.
It is beautiful.

Part One

GENESIS TO JOHN

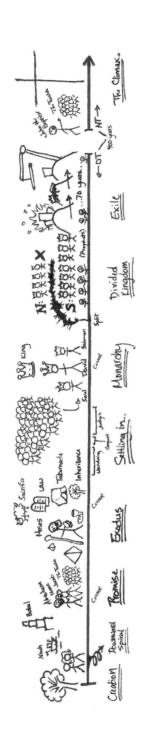

01 creation

The Bible begins with a song. It has an opening number—the first chapter of **Genesis** could very well be considered the Bible's overture. The first words about our universe's origin, ordering, and purpose come to us in poetry. What else could do justice to our marvelous Creator and his expansive, jaw-dropping universe?

All is void. All is empty darkness.

God speaks and brings light.[1] That will be the pattern of the story. This is what God absolutely loves doing. It's the kind of God he is.

With infectious and joyous rhythm, the Creator separates light from dark, sky from sea, land from water. What was a void of emptiness and chaos beings exploding with creative energy: proteins and porcupines, comets and constellations, waterfalls and wildflowers. Beauty and life burst onto the scene.

Day One, it's good.
Day Two, it's good.
Day Three, it's good.

That's the rhythm—the beat, the chorus—of the song.[2]

---

[1] Gen 1:2-3.
[2] Gen 1:3, 9, 12, 18, 21, 25.

There was only chaos and lifelessness until we find God—through his spoken Word and ever-present Spirit—bringing order and life.

As the music climbs toward its crescendo
and the poem approaches its climax,
God creates something utterly unique:

Humanity.

The human race stands apart from the rest of the world in both its essence and its purpose—what humanity *is* and what humanity *does*.

And these two things are linked:

Humanity resembles God in an utterly unique way. We're stamped with God's image and charged with caring for the amazing world just sung into existence.[3] Our humanity stems from sharing God's character and acting on God's behalf.

To be human, in a real sense, is to be like God. Human beings are walking, talking "images" of God. We are christened as God's representatives in the world.[4]

The song crescendos with the seventh day, with God resting from his work and simply enjoying relationship with his creation.[5]

The Creator communes with his creation.
The creation enjoys its Creator.

---

[3] Gen 1:27.
[4] Gen 1:28. (see also Psalm 89.)
[5] Gen 2:1-3.

Humanity enters joy and rest in the God who fashioned them in his own image. We discover our destiny by enjoying relationship with him and serving as the caretakers of his creation.

Things are good.

Scratch that. Things are *very good*.[6]

In this seemingly simple overture, the Bible makes a revolutionary claim —there is only one God and this God is all-powerful. Western culture has been so shaped by Genesis (whether or not we are "believers") that we hardly recognize the audacity of this assertion:

First, Genesis assumes there is only one God. The countless gods, deities, and divine forces so prominent in other ancient creation stories of other cultures find no place here. Those stories often depict the universe as the chance by-product of violence and bloodshed between the gods.[7] But the God of Genesis does not struggle against anyone or anything else.

The Creator is The-One-and-The-Only.

This is a one-God-show.
Unequaled and unchallenged.

This leads naturally into the second gigantic assertion of this opening song—this God has absolute power. He does not *try* to create anything. Rather, he *accomplishes* everything exactly as he wants. He speaks, it happens.

---

6 Gen 1:31.

7 Try googling other ancient creation stories such as the Babylonian Enuma Elish. The violence and multitude of finite gods contrast sharply with the monotheistic poem of sovereign goodness found here in Genesis.

Genesis' first chapter insists that behind all things there is one good, all-powerful Creator. There is only one God. And this God is sovereign.

This God is King.

The revolutionary idea of monotheism,[8] so foundational to the beginning of Scripture, is incredibly good news. It means that neither creation nor history are a mistake. The world does not emerge from a roll of the dice —this Creator *intentionally* creates. Chaos and chance are not at the root of reality—they are not the bedrock of the universe. Creating and sustaining everything, we are the joy and goodness of one, all-powerful God.

The Genesis Overture sets the stage for what's coming.

There's only one God... the King.

Humanity is not a mistake,
we reflect God's character.

Humanity is not adrift,
we are to partner with the Creator.

Humanity is not alone,
we are to commune with our King.

It's good, it's good, it's very good.

The music begins to fade...
now the *story* of the Bible begins.[9]

---

[8] Monotheism comes from two Greek words: mono (meaning "only") and theos (meaning "god").
[9] Gen 2:4 begins a second account of creation that compliments the first. The song gives way to the story. And the story uses the same opening words ("this is the account") as Gen 5:1, 10:1 & 11:10.

God and dirt.

We might think this an unlikely pair, but this is the way the story begins. The creation of humanity gets described again, this time in more earthy terms. God is pictured as carving the Man ("adam" in Hebrew) from the dusty ground ("adam-ah" in Hebrew).

In the Overture, humanity is made in God's image. God created humanity in his image, *male and female he created them*.[10]

Here the Story expresses this same truth in a different way: humans are dirt filled with God's very breath and spirit.[11]

God gives this "mud-man" (or "dirt-dude" or "earthling," take your pick) responsibility to care for God's very own garden and creation.[12] With this gift, God gives him meaning and purpose.

The one-from-the-land is given land.

Humanity will arrange, order, govern and enjoy creation.[13]

Consider that: work and responsibility are built into our existence.

Our culture often idealizes an early retirement free from work and responsibility, but both are God-given. Both are an integral part of what it means to be human. They are gifts before rebellion or corruption or death enter the story. Creation is good and so are work and responsibility, despite their reputations in popular culture.

---

10 Gen 1:27.
11 Gen 2:7.
12 Gen 2:8-15.
13 Gen 2:15-16.

Meaning, purpose, and (ultimately) joy come from participating in the work and responsibility of God.

This work and responsibility brings us to a huge assumption embedded throughout the Bible's story: God has given humanity freedom to choose whether they will live as he designed.

"But you must not" follows and assumes *"You are free to eat."*[14]

Responsibility assumes freedom.

Our freedom stands right next to our all-powerful Creator. God is the supreme sovereign but the puppet-master. The universe is not some kind of cosmic game with the divine moving humanity as pawns. It is real relationship between the living God and his living people. The all-powerful King grants real freedom to his subjects.

The Bible often embraces "both/and" where we want "either/or."

We have been given the gift of choice.
Real freedom allows real relationship with God.

God is good.
Creation is good.

Work and responsibility are good.
Freedom is good.

It's good, it's good, it's very good.

The LORD God said, "It is not good..."

---

14 Gen 2:16-17.

Whoa—wait a second! We're still in the garden of delight![15] Not good!? We better pay close attention—this is important. The Man has been reflecting God's image, using his freedom in all the right ways, ordering creation, naming animals, and enjoying the garden and its Creator...

But something's still not right.

Something is not good.
"It is not good for man to be alone."[16]

Essential to being human is the need for relationship.
To know others and to be known.

Straight from the lips of God: we are not meant to be alone. We are meant for relationship. We are meant for community.

God gives a partner to the Man—from a chunk of the Man's side, God creates a "matching strength" for the Man.[17]

God creates the Woman.

The picture here is of the Man and the Woman united and equal in responsibility, work, and status. That's precisely why the Man bursts into a love song: *"This is now bone of my bones and flesh of my flesh."*[18] He has to sing—he is overjoyed, captivated and delighted to find a matching strength.

---

[15] In Hebrew, Eden literally means "delight."
[16] Gen 2:18.
[17] In the words of Matthew Henry: "That the woman was *made of a rib out of the side of Adam;* not made out of his head to rule over him, nor out of his feet to be trampled upon by him, but out of his side to be equal with him, under his arm to be protected, and near his heart to be beloved." Matthew Henry, *Matthew Henry's Commentary on the Whole Bible, Volume I (Genesis to Deuteronomy).*
[18] Gen 2:23.

Here is a true partner who is nothing like the beasts surrounding him. She is gloriously like him except with lovelier features, nicer hair, and better fashion sense.

With that, Genesis 2 comes to an absolutely blissful conclusion: *The man and his wife were both naked and they felt no shame.*[19]

This simple sentence has haunted readers for millennia, reaching deep into the imaginations of our hearts about what relationships, life, and the world ought to look like.

No clothes, that much is obvious.
But the imagery is not merely skin-deep.

No barriers, no pretending, no posturing.

Here we find human relationship without masks, without lies, and without anxiety. Nothing to hide and nothing to fear. They are naked and feel no shame.

Community and relationships flourish in this garden—along with everything else. The Man and the Woman are fully known by God and fully known by each other.

This garden, this work, this freedom, this life, this God…
everything is delight.

All is gift.
All is grace.

---

[19] Gen 2:25.

This is what it looks like when the good Creator reigns as King over creation with his people. The reign of this God is good.

It's good, it's good, it's very good.

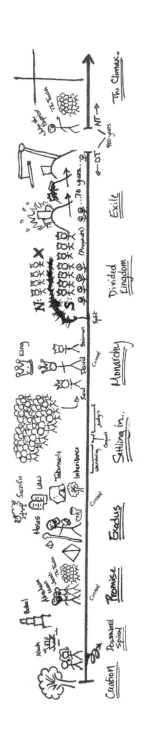

02 downward spiral

The opening two chapters of Genesis tell the origins and purpose of creation. The omnipotent One-and-Only fashions humanity in his own image to be free for real responsibility and real relationship. Under the reign of this Creator, humanity will care for and rule over creation. All of creation is so very good.

But the next nine chapters
are where things unravel.[1]

The tragedy of creation's downfall begins with an infamous story about a forbidden tree and a cunning serpent. The Man and the Woman are enticed by this serpent into distrusting and disobeying their Creator.[2]

You see, when God placed the first couple in the garden of delight only one stipulation was given. They must not eat from a particular tree: the tree of the knowledge of good and evil.[3] They are free for everything else. For work and rest, for eating and love-making, for enjoying the garden and the animals and the company of each other.

Who could possibly want more?

The answer is "We could."

---

[1] Gen 3-11.
[2] Gen 3:1-24.
[3] Gen 2:16-17.

The serpent succeeds in convincing the Woman (and we might also note the Man *who was with her*[4]) that they would become "like God" if only they will eat this forbidden fruit. A better reality than the one you've been given is only one compromise away.

The tragic irony, of course, is they are *already* created in God's image. They are *already* an embodied reflection of the Creator himself to each other and all of creation. They are *already* like God in glorious and profound ways.[5] But this is not enough for them.

They decide to believe that their Creator is holding out on them, that there is more life elsewhere, that they can create a better reality than the one given to them.[6] This story would be better if they were its authors.

So they disobey. They distrust. They eat the fruit.

They embrace themselves as supreme.
They choose lies over truth.
They rebel against the reign of the King.

This infamous tale—old and familiar as it is—remains new and illuminating because it focuses on the "why" of the world as it is.

Why is the world in the terrible condition that it is?
Why is there evil if there is an all-powerful and good God?

Why does the unnatural horror of death stain everything?

---

4 Gen 3:6.

5 Psalm 8.

6 I find this quote extraordinarily helpful: "The God of Genesis is characterized in part by the pleasure he takes in what he has made. 'And God saw that it was good.' The worldview of the envious – and to a certain extent, of the lustful and avaricious too – runs counter to God's vision. Nothing they see is good, or good enough, or else nothing they see is enough of the good. In other words, you can never please them, which is as good a definition as you may get of what it means to be damned," Garret Keizer, *The Enigma of Anger*, 46.

Why corruption? Why suffering? Why rebellion? Why hatred?

The story offers us a terrible, sobering answer... we are the why.

The real freedom and responsibility God gave humanity also carried a real danger. Humanity might use their freedom to disobey. They could choose to rebel against God's reign. They could choose a reality apart from his good design—a reality dominated by suffering and corruption and darkness and death.

As C.S. Lewis writes, "Of course God knew what would happen if they used their freedom the wrong way: apparently He thought it worth the risk."[7]

To have real, meaningful relationship with his divinely-infused-dirt, this all-powerful God made room for their choices.

And they are making the wrong choices.

Humanity chooses insurrection against the universe's King.

We chose—and frequently still choose—to exercise our freedom in self-centered, self-promoting and (finally) self-destroying ways. This is one of the points driven home by the story of forbidden fruit. One scholar writes that this story "wishes to indicate very simply that evil is a human product, that God created the world good but that man, through the free exercise of his will in rebellion against God, corrupts the good and puts evil in its place."[8]

Why is the world in the condition it is?

7 C.S. Lewis, *Mere Christianity* (New York: Harper Collins, 2001), 46.
8 Nahum Sarna, *Understanding Genesis* (New York: Shocken Books, 1966), 24.

Because we wanted it that way.
Or at least we wanted it *our* way.

The holy rhythm of Scripture's overture ("it's good, it's good") has been interrupted by the rusty rattling of rebellion. And suddenly the story begins spiraling downward in a direction we're much more familiar with. It begins to resemble what we experience—darkness in the world and darkness within ourselves.

The story of the Bible
begins to sound like a tragedy.

But this was an perfectly predictable tragedy. After all, God had warned how disobedience and rebellion would be death-dealing.[9] And this makes perfect sense:

When a flowering tree is uprooted from its soil, no one is shocked when it withers and dies. The same is true of deepest levels of reality. God warns that rebellion will (naturally and justly) lead to death.

Rebelling against the King kills us as surely as a tree without soil.

We uprooted ourselves and rejected life.
It was good, it was good, and so much still is.

But now humanity has rebelled.

God's intentions have been interrupted.
Creation has been corrupted.

Hatred has appeared. Evil has entered.

---

9 Gen 2:17.

Death has begun its rule and reign.

The Man and the Woman wanted to be gods in themselves, and they've plunged creation into a nightmare. So God will explain what the universe will look like under the cursed consequences of human rebellion.

But we can already see it before God can say a word:

A curse begins infecting humanity before our eyes—a rift opens in the first relationship. When asked about his actions, the Man responds, *"The woman you put here with me—she gave me some fruit from the tree, and I ate it."*[10]

Finger pointing, accusations flying, blame shifting.

Gut-wrenching. Heart-breaking.
A far cry from naked and unashamed.

And when we examine the Man's words carefully, his blame of the Woman is ultimately aimed at God. It's ultimately God's gift and God Himself that's the problem. Horror grows as we realize the rift between the Man and the Woman is only evidence of a rupture in their relationship with their Maker.

The Man and the Woman no longer trust God or each other. By refusing to be honest—they both freely rebelled—they continue to live in that rebellion. Neither coerced the other, and now they're willing to sacrifice relationship to escape responsibility.

---

10 Gen 3:12.

God finally speaks, cursing both the ground and the serpent. The land so beautifully designed and described[11] will now produce thorns and thistles, briars and barbs.[12] The earth's fruit will reflect its fall. The snake is humiliated to slither in the dirt below the earth's vulgar vegetation.[13]

(And from this point forward, the serpent becomes one of the Bible's primary symbols of evil and of its animosity toward humankind.)

But a chord of hope
can be heard
under this chorus of curses.

The offspring of the Woman will crush the serpent's head, and the serpent will only manage to strike his foot.[14]

Evil will wound, but it will never win.

In this early (albeit vague) prophecy, hope is proclaimed. The serpent— suddenly a central symbol of evil plaguing creation—will eventually be vanquished.

In addition to curses and prophecy, God also explains that pain will now pervade the human experience. The Woman's pain will be rooted in child-bearing, the Man's pain rooted in toilsome labor.[15] God tells how the Woman (intended to be a "matching strength" for the Man) will wind up being ruled over by him.[16]

---

11 Gen 2:10-14.
12 Gen 3:17-18.
13 Gen 3:14.
14 Gen 3:15b.
15 Gen 3:16 and 3:19.
16 Gen 3:16b. God is describing—not endorsing—a coming rift in their relationship.

The beautiful, co-creative power of human reproduction will now become dangerous. The delight of meaningful work will now grow heavy and burdensome. Outside of Eden, what was once good and life-giving becomes toilsome and tainted by death.

God's good gifts have become twisted.
Good creation has fallen far.

And things continue their downward spiral as chapters unfold.

The terrifying ramifications of humanity's "fall" continue in the shocking story of Cain and Abel—the first two sons of the Man and the Woman (remembered as Adam and Eve).[17] Cain works as a herdsman, and Abel works as a farmer. Both offer sacrifices to God, yet God only accepts Abel's sacrifice. Cain's sacrifice is not accepted. We're not told why— their responses are the point of the story. Cain murders his brother Abel in his anger.[18]

The blaming, division and fracture of the parents has blossomed into jealousy, rage and murder in their children. When God asks where Abel is, Cain darkly replies with another question: *"Am I my brother's keeper?"*[19] Obviously not. The children of Adam have begun to slay their siblings instead of caring for them.

God can hear Abel's blood crying out from the ground.

The blood cries "injustice." It cries out against Cain.
Life is so precious that Abel's murderer must be cursed.[20]

---

17 Adam (still literally "the Man") names Eve in Genesis 3:20.
18 Gen 4:1-8.
19 Gen 4:9b.
20 Gen 4:10. (See too Gen 9:6)

The story now transitions into another familiar story, this one centering on a man named Noah, an ark, his family and a worldwide flood. This is not, however, a cute, family-friendly cartoon about all our favorite animals on one big boat.

This is some of the darkest stuff in the Bible.

Noah's story actually begins by the tracing of two legacies—Cain's family and Adam's family. Cain's family becomes progressively darker and more corrupt.[21] Adam's legacy on the other hand (carried on by another son named Seth) leads us to Noah—an upright and blameless man.[22] But Noah's moral character cannot stem the tide of corruption surging through Cain's family. The Humanity's primal rebellion comes to dominate the earth:

The LORD saw how the wickedness of the human race had become on the earth, and that every inclination of the thoughts of the human heart was only evil all the time.[23]

Notice the incredibly sweeping language here:

Every—Only—All.

It's not good. It's not good. Not good at all.

So God resolves to purge corruption from his creation with a flood. We might notice how this is quite unlike flood narratives from other ancient cultures. In those stories, the gods choose to flood the earth almost on a whim or for rather trivial reasons.[24] Not so in this story:

---

[21] Gen 4:17-26. The legacy climaxes with Lamech's song in v23-24, bragging about killing a man over a trifle and how he would need to be avenged more than his ancestor Cain.

[22] Gen 5 and Gen 6:9. Notice how the genealogy of Genesis 5 reminds us that things are not good with its repetition of death.

[23] Gen 6:5b.

[24] For instance, in Epic of Gilgamesh the god Enlil decides that the human race is far too noisy for his tastes.

God cannot allow evil to go unchecked.
God must act.

God's decision here is rooted in his justice.
God must destroy what destroys good creation.

After all, he is a *good* God—any sense of justice we have in us is ultimately a mere shadow of his heart.

The despicable levels to which humanity stooped calls for a drastic action to conquer the chaos and restore goodness. If we take this dark story seriously on its own terms, we can only thank God for the flood.

Every—Only—All.

Thank God that our Creator is also a Judge—the world needed one. And countless injustices we see around us today testify that the world still needs one.

God chooses Noah and family to be his people, saving them through water.[25] After this dramatic rescue, God blesses them with words that echo God's earliest blessings on humanity.[26]

But this turns out to be a fresh start on a stained slate.
God purged evil from the earth but not from the human heart.[27]

If this were a film, the camera has been progressively pulling back. The scope of the scene has grown wider and wider since the goodness of Eden shattered:

---

25 The familiar story of Noah and the flood is found in Gen 6:9-9:17.
26 Compare (and also contrast!) Gen 9:1-7 with Gen 1:28-29.
27 Gen 8:21

Cain and Abel shocked us with the new dark realities.
Familial disputes. Conflicting vocations.

Humanity has the capacity
both to create life and destroy life.

The legacies of Cain and Adam (told through genealogies) shows the story spreading like a web across centuries.

Now with the rescue of Noah and his family through the flood, our gaze has expanded to include the entire earth.

Which brings us to the story of the Tower of Babel.[28]

At this point, the view is so wide that our main characters have become "the nations" rather than individuals. These nations come together in willful rebellion against God's desire for the entire earth to be filled.[29] They arrogantly conspire to make a great name for themselves in one central location.[30] They plot to build a grand tower that will unify them and reach the heavens.

The root of humanity's rebellion remains constant:
humanity still wants to be God.

This time in fame and reputation... and altitude.

The scene plays out with incredible irony. God—in the very heavens they're trying to reach—must venture downward to examine their "tall" tower.[31] And in response to the nations' rebellion, he confuses their

---

28 Gen 11:1-9.
29 Gen 1:28, 9:1.
30 Gen 11:4.
31 Gen 11:5, 7.

languages. (According to the story, they had all spoken the same "tongue" up to now.[32])

Suddenly these ambitious architects can no longer communicate with each other. They're all just babbling at each other. The babble eventually causes the entire project to be scrapped as humanity dissolves into factions.

So that place was called Babel.

Aside from being a delightfully biting satire on Babylon's origins,[33] this story provides a bookend for the downward spiral which began in Genesis 3.

The lens has been widening, showcasing how corruption has spread through every level of human existence:

Interpersonal relationships are fracturing
between the Man and the Woman.

Family bonds are decaying into murder
with the first brothers.

Wickedness has begun filling societies.
Injustice begins dominating cultures.

The pride of "progress" winds up splintering the nations.

Darkness, sin, corruption and death have spread like a virus from the personal to the family and finally to all societies world-wide.

---

[32] Gen 11:1.
[33] Gen 11:9. Babylon proudly told a very different sort of tale where their city's name meant "gate of gods." Here it evidently implies something like "confusion" or "incompetence."

With this wide-angle lens, the story pans across a grim scene. The King's good creation smolders in wreckage spanning from Cain to Babel. We need hope that things can be restored. We need a promise that God has not abandoned creation.

Well, we're in luck.
We're about to zoom in for a close-up and get both.

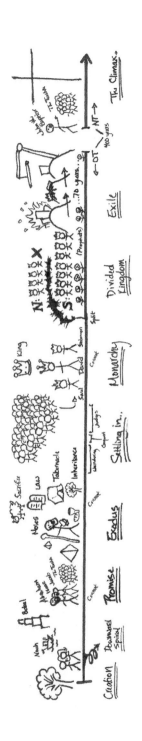

03 promise

The human race has taken creation wildly off course. The subjects charged with caring for the kingdom have rebelled against the King. Mankind has infected the world with a curse, and their rejection of God's reign is corroding every level of existence.

Relationships ruin, families fracture, society splinters.
Everything and everyone dies.
Death reigns everywhere.

The camera has just finished surveying the tattered remains of creation, with "the nations" starring now as our rebellious, broken characters.[1]

The world is hemorrhaging and needs divine triage.

What will God do? How will God act?
How will God renew creation?

Enter God's promise to a man named Abraham.

We are introduced to Abraham and his wife Sarah (originally named Abram and Sarai[2]) as they are departing from the familiar homeland of

---

[1] Framed especially by the "Table of Nations" in Genesis 10 and story of Babel's tower in Genesis 11.
[2] Their names are changed in Gen 17:5, 15.

46

Abraham's father. God has called, and they're leaving the land of Ur and heading to the land of Canaan.[3]

God chooses Abraham out of obscurity. He's a nobody special. There's nothing remarkable about Abraham other than the fact that God chooses him. He had two brothers—Haran and Nahor. Why didn't God choose them?[4] Why don't three major religions (Judaism, Christianity and Islam) talk about "Father Haran" or "Father Nahor" instead of "Father Abraham"?

We're not told. And God is free to do that.

God can choose whom he wants to choose.
God can elect whom he wants for the task of saving the world.

Here's how God introduces himself to Abraham:

"I will make you into a great nation, and I will bless you; I will make your name great, and you will be a blessing. I will bless those who bless you, and whoever curses you I will curse; and all peoples on earth will be blessed through you."[5]

How's that for an icebreaker?

Nice to meet you, Abraham. I've got this little plan for you...

This is a huge promise, especially in light of the story that came right before it. The nations have recently been thrown to the wind for wanting to make a great name for themselves. And now here's God promising to

---

[3] Located in modern-day Iraq. Abraham is actually coming from the area that will centuries later be known as "Babylon."
[4] Gen 11:27.
[5] Gen 12:2-3.

build Abraham into a nation (with a great name!) for the sake of those self-destructive nations.

Evidently great names and blessing are part of God's plan.
We just keep wanting to define the terms.

So God plans will make Abraham into this great and vast nation whose descendants will be like the countless stars in the sky.[6] You might think that one huge promise was enough, but you would be wrong. God continues to dish out the grand promises:

God will give Abraham's family the land called Canaan as an inheritance.[7] The eastern shore of the Mediterranean will be his strategic staging ground for blessing the world. Abraham's descendants will be God's people, and he will be their God.[8]

And to seal the deal, as it where, God gives Abraham and all his male descendants an intimate, earthy reminder of these promises:

Circumcision.[9]

Abraham might have forgotten a handshake… but not this.

These grand promises are part of a covenant (or agreement or contract) that God is making with Abraham. There are no strings attached here. Abraham has done nothing to earn these promises and there is nothing Abraham can do to secure them. God has put himself—and himself alone—on the hook to keep these promises.

---

[6] Gen 15:5.
[7] Gen 15:7.
[8] Gen 17:8.
[9] Gen 17:9-14.

This is a one-sided deal to bless the world.

Just sit back and watch.

God is not choosing Abraham—not *electing* Abraham—so that Abraham can sit around with a big, stupid smile and congratulate himself for being chosen. No, being chosen by God always means chosen for a *purpose*:

To bring blessing to the broken world.

God elects Abraham for the sake of the world.

The King intends to heal his hemorrhaging creation *through* his rebellious subjects. And true to the freedom he gave them, God consistently chooses to work through humanity.

Get used to hearing about Abraham and his family because the rest of the Bible has them near its center. Scripture's story follows their deeds and misdeeds, their fortunes and failings, their belief and unbelief, their exodus and exile.

God will use them to bless this broken world.

Are you aching to finally hear the words, "it's good, it's good" again?

Well, the Bible places all its bets on Abraham's family.

Alright—blessing the world through Abraham's family. Well this immediately raises questions about precisely *how* God is going to do that. The most immediate, practical question that fills the story with dramatic tension concerns Abraham's barren wife. Because well… that's it in a nutshell: Sarah is barren.[10]

Sarah's infertility is a punch in the stomach. It reminds us of the curse plaguing creation. Things are not right in the world, and so things are not right in Sarah. God originally meant for humanity to be blessed with plenty of children,[11] but their rebellion meant there would be pain, danger and difficulty in this actually happening.[12]

And Sarah is more than just barren.
Sarah is old. Quite old.
Quite like Abraham.

She's been barren for a long time.

Infertility in our world today is heart-breaking. But in the world of the ancient near east, infertility was society-breaking. Families were sprawling political units. To be barren meant to be cursed by the gods because it also meant no heirs, limited economic viability and no lasting legacy.

None of this is exactly helpful for a guy who's supposed to be blessing the world. Yet to this geriatric, infertile couple we find God dealing out promises of heirs, land and cosmic blessing.

No wonder Sarah laughs at God.[13]

Old, barren women do not give birth.

---

10 Gen 11:30.
11 Gen 1:28; 9:1, 7.
12 Gen 3:16a.
13 Gen 18:9-15.

A second question compounding Sarah's infertility and age is the unscrupulous nature of her husband: Abraham is something of a scoundrel. Scripture hardly portrays him—or any other biblical character —in the pristine, sparkling way we might expect from the reverence shown to him today by Jews, Christians and Muslims.

Abraham twice hands his wife Sarah over to powerful men for his own personal gain.[14] He sleeps with their Egyptian slave (at his wife's suggestion) to gain an heir without Sarah.[15] He banishes that slave (and their child!) into the desert after Sarah finally gives birth to a son.[16]

Some of these stories can be—and rightfully should be—chalked up to cultural differences. But many parts cannot.

Abraham is hardly a moral beacon of light.
Yet God chooses him and makes him cosmic promises.

Faults and all.

And Abraham trusts God. He takes God at his word.

In spite of his character defects,
Abraham fiercely believes God.

And trusting this God is precisely what counts.[17]

Sarah does eventually give Abraham a son. Remembering how she chuckled at the outrageous promises of God, Abraham and Sarah name their son "Laughter." That is, they name him Isaac.

---

14 Gen 12:11-16; 20:1-2.
15 Gen 16:1-4.
16 Gen 21:1-20.
17 Gen 15:6.

No one is laughing, however, when God tells Abraham to take Isaac to a mountain and sacrifice him.[18] Sacrifice Isaac!? We are shocked and appalled, but readers throughout many generations were not. This was standard fare of the day. The gods of the ancient world frequently demanded the sacrifice of children, especially first-borns.[19]

This God is evidently just like all the others and (quite reasonably) wants Abraham's first-born son. If this God is powerful enough to give a scoundrel and his barren wife an heir in their old age, he is certainly powerful enough to do it again.

But the dues must be paid.
After all, the gods need sacrifices.

No surprise, Abraham starts to follow the instructions…
…huge surprise, God stops him.

This God is different, and he's made his point.
This is a God who provides the sacrifice himself.[20]

Isaac lives to carry the promise of hope placed on Abraham's family forward. As the story unfolds, we notice patterns following one generation to the next, much like families today. Isaac courts and marries a woman named Rebekah, who is also barren.[21]

And God provides an heir yet again—this time twins!

---

[18] Gen 22:1-19.
[19] See Lev 18:21; Jer 19:5 for examples of two gods (Molek and Baal) who demanded this.
[20] Gen 22:8.
[21] Gen 25:21.

The older twin Esau emerges first, his brother literally grabbing at his heel.[22] In that culture, the oldest son was extraordinarily important. As firstborn, the legacy of the family will continue through Esau. Families focused their collective resources on one son to ensure the economic and political continuation of the family. Good thing too—we certainly need for someone to carry on this particular family's legacy:

This family will be as vast as the stars in the sky!
This family will inherit the land of Canaan!
This family will be God's means of blessing the entire world!

Thank God for Esau!

But God surprises again.

He gave an heir despite biological and moral deficiencies.
He just wants to be trusted.

He defied all expectations of what he should demand as "a god." He just wants to be trusted.

Now, he's about to operate counter-culturally.
He'll work through the two-timing, second-born runt of the family.

Maybe we should trust him.

The name of this two-timing second-born runt is Jacob.

Jacob is a fascinating character-study in deceit.[23]

---

22 Gen 25:24-26.
23 "Jacob" in Hebrew literally means "he deceives."

The man is a regular con-artist.

If Abraham was a scoundrel,
Jacob is a snake.

For instance, he extorts Esau out of his "first-born son privileges" with a bowl of lentil stew.[24] This means that Jacob now will get the first-born's portion of the estate (two-thirds) when Isaac dies. Its a stupid thing for Esau to give up, but it's a horrifying thing for Jacob to take.

In another instance, Jacob dresses up in Esau's clothes to trick Isaac— now old and blind—into blessing him instead of Esau.[25] Jacob intercepts his father's blessing, an profoundly significant and symbolic cultural event in the life of first-born son.

That's the last straw. The camel's back has broken.
Esau swears that as soon as their father dies, so will Jacob.[26]

Esau does not, however, get an opportunity to reenact Cain and Abel. At the prodding of his mother, Jacob flees the region and goes to live with her brother, Laban.

On his way, God appears to Jacob in a dream and reconfirms the promises that had been made to Grandpa Abraham: *"I am the LORD, the God of your father Abraham and the God of Isaac. I will give you and your descendants the land on which you are lying. Your descendants will be like the dust of the earth, and you will spread out to the west and to the east, to the north and to the south. All peoples on earth will be blessed through you and your offspring."*[27]

---

24 Gen 25:29-34.
25 Gen 27:1-40.
26 Gen 27:41.
27 Gen 28:13-14.

Jacob is stunned. So are we.

Evidently God has elected this two-timing, second-born runt who has swindled and conned at every turn as the one through whom he'll bring blessing.

Jacob decides that if this God can carry him safely back to his father's household (he's headed the opposite direction, mind you), then he'll claim this God as his own.[28] And with that decision, Jacob continues on and settles down with Uncle Laban. During his time there, he finds love and fortune, and both come hard.

Jacob falls for Laban's daughter Rachel,[29] but ends up being conned (ironically in very similar fashion to the disguise-stunt he pulled on his dad) into marrying Rachel's older sister. The trickster has been tricked. The conman conned. After committing himself to several more years of manual labor, Jacob finally wins Rachel's hand as well.[30]

Jacob secures his fortune with equal drama. As Jacob works for him, Uncle Laban tries hard to swindle him out of money. But Jacob wins this battle too—with a double-dose of cunning and a good bit of selective livestock breeding.[31]

By the time we arrive in Genesis 31, Jacob has siphoned off most of Laban's riches, married both his daughters and is fleeing for his life once again.

The story is funny. It's right to laugh.
This is a family of scoundrels, cheats and thieves.

---

[28] Gen 28:20-22.
[29] Marriage between cousins was common practice in the ancient near east as a means of keeping family blood "pure."
[30] Gen 29:15-30.
[31] Gen 30:25-43.

Jacob finally returns, reconciles with Esau and travels back to his father's household. He's back in the land promised to Abraham. And since he came back safely, Jacob plans to claim the promise-making God of his grandfather as his own.

Instead, this God ends up claiming Jacob.

God does this by renaming him. His grandfather Abram was renamed Abraham. The identity originally given to Jacob—the deceiver—will not define him.

Jacob is renamed Israel.[32]

Now the story shifts its attention to the twelve sons of Israel. They are all cunning and clever men, much like their father. Among them are memorable names like Benjamin, Levi and Judah. But almost immediately overshadowing all of them is Joseph. And his story is arguably one of the most famous in the Bible.

If you squash this masterful story into a paragraph, you get this:

Joseph is Israel's favorite son which makes all his brothers incredibly jealous. They conspire to kill Joseph but settle for selling him into slavery. Joseph winds up in Egypt, the economic and military superpower of the day. Because God is with him, he rises the ranks of an important man's household but winds up unjustly imprisoned. Because God is with him, he rises the ranks of prison but must wait there for years. Because God is with him, he is able to interpret the disturbing dreams of Pharaoh, the superpower's king. The dreams warn of a devastating famine which will cripple Egypt and the entire region after seven years of prosperity.

---

[32] Gen 35:9-15 (see also 32:22-32). "Israel" means "he struggles with God." A fitting name for the people of God to be remembered by.

Joseph's wisdom makes him ideal to develop and execute a plan for storing and rationing food during the next fourteen years. This food feeds not only Egypt but also the surrounding nations. To top it off, during the height of this regional crisis, Joseph's brothers come to Egypt searching for food. After a game of cat-and-mouse to see how their character has developed over the years, Joseph reveals himself to them. They're all reconciled, and the entire family (including good old Israel himself) comes to Egypt.[33]

Whew—that's quite the tale.

Joseph himself seems to recognize the significance and meaning of his own experiences: *"You intended to harm me, but God intended it for good to accomplish what is now being done, the saving of many lives."*[34]

His words are some of the last in the book of Genesis. As the book closes, Israel and his twelve sons are safe and prosperous in Egypt along with all their wives, children, servants and livestock. Israel's favorite son has been through hell, but God is working all things out for good.

The reality of God's providence stands out as a significant theme in Joseph's story. God steers the darkest of human choices toward good—which is unbelievably good news. Maybe there's hope that the Creator will also work the corruption of his creation for good.

Perhaps he's that powerful.
Perhaps he's that good.

---

[33] Gen 37:1-47:12.
[34] Gen 50:20.

Abraham's family has grown and is now blessing the world through Joseph in Egypt.

Could this be the fulfilling God's promises?

If so, why isn't Abraham's family in the land of promise?
And they're not exactly like the stars of the sky yet, are they?

This giving of bread to the nations is like a shadow of some bigger, coming blessing. God will indeed bless the nations through Abraham's family, but there's quite a bit more story to be told.

This is, after all, just the end of Genesis.

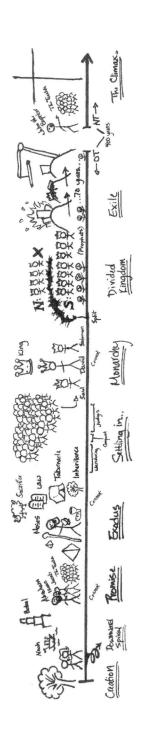

04 the exodus

Mankind mangled has a masterpiece. The good creation spiraled into darkness, its Artist promised he would set things right.

The Creator made a covenant—a binding deal—with a man named Abraham to bless the world through his family. By the end of Genesis, this family is sitting pretty in Egypt, the superpower of the day, blessing the nations through the wisdom of Joseph. He and his brothers (and their twelve families) grow and prosper in Egypt. They eventually pass away, leaving new generations of "Israelites" (as they will be called) in their place.[1]

But *then a new king,*
to whom Joseph meant nothing,
came to power in Egypt.[2]

These ominous words foreshadow
the turn our story is about to take.

The banks of the Nile have been an oasis of security for Jacob, his sons and their families. After all, Joseph had been second in the land only to the pharaoh. But after four centuries, Egypt is no longer safe.[3]

---

[1] Ex 1:1-7.
[2] Ex 1:8.
[3] Ex 12:40-42 says that it was 430 years (cf. Gal 3:17).

This new king forgets how Joseph (and his God) had saved Egypt from national disaster. And this short national memory combines with concern about the swelling ranks of these Israelites—how they may affect the national and economic security of the nation.[4]

"The Israelites have become far too numerous for us."[5]

The ambition and ingenuity of ancient Egypt still marvels us today. Massive pyramids, colossal statues and great obelisks all punctuate an otherwise desolate landscape. This "Israelite crisis" provided another chance to creatively expand their empire. Under the reign of this new Pharaoh, the Egyptians subject the Israelites to forced labor. The Israelites become slaves.

But they continue to grow even in their bondage.
The banks of the Nile are flooding with Abraham's children.

And *so the Egyptians came to dread the Israelites and worked them ruthlessly. They made their lives bitter with harsh labor in brick and mortar and with all kinds of work in the fields; in all their harsh labor the Egyptians worked them ruthlessly.*[6]

The thundering skies of **Exodus** have replaced the bright horizon at the end of Genesis. As the black clouds roll in, however, God reveals another aspect of his character. Up to this point, God has revealed himself in several different ways:

As Creator.
As Judge.
As Promise-maker.

---

[4] Ex 1:10.
[5] Ex 1:9.
[6] Ex 1:12b-14.

But we're about to meet him as Redeemer.

The God who unchains captives.
The God who liberates the oppressed.
The God who releases slaves from bondage.

God is about to introduce himself like this to a man named Moses.

When we first meet baby Moses, he's immediately in danger. Among the nasty orders of this new (and nameless) Pharaoh's, we find a decree to kill all male Israelite infants.[7] Moses' parents rescue him, however, from this fate launching him down the Nile on his own baby-sized ark.[8] The Pharaoh's very own daughter winds up rescuing him from the river.

So the very person God will use to break Pharaoh's pride and power receives nurture and care under his very nose.[9] And though Moses grows up in Pharaoh's house, we can recognize in him a passion for justice mirroring God's own. It's this hatred of injustice that drives Moses to kill an Egyptian he sees abusing an Israelite. After that, he has to skip town as a fugitive.[10]

With Egypt fading in his rear-view mirror, Moses settles down with a group of people in the land of Midian. There he starts a family and becomes a shepherd.[11] All the while, however, the rest of his fellow Israelites continue to suffer in Egyptian chains and continue to cry out to God.

---

7 Ex 1:16 is the first order that is brilliantly subverted by two Hebrew midwives, whose names we are given: Shiphrah and Puah. This stands in striking contrast to the Pharaoh, who is slighted in the text by withholding his name. The second order, given in Ex 1:22 may have been harder to stop.
8 Intriguing note: the Hebrew word for "basket" used in Ex 2:3, 5 is the same word used to describe what Noah built.
9 Ex 2:5-10.
10 Ex 2:11-15.
11 Ex 2:16-22.

And God hears those cries. That's the kind of God he is.

He remembers his promises to Abraham, Isaac and Jacob. His promise to bless them and to bless the world through them. And it is time to act.

It is time to bring this massive group of families—this chosen people— out of slavery and into this land of promise so that all the nations can be blessed through them. Moses, with his deep (but mishandled) sense of justice, will do nicely as God's agent for this task.

On a mountain called Sinai, God appears to Moses in an iconic moment —the burning bush. God says that he has heard the cry of his oppressed people—he has not forgotten them. And he is now sending Moses to this new Pharaoh to deliver the Israelites out of slavery.[12]

Moses doesn't want the job. With excuse after excuse, Moses resists God's design for him. Sound familiar?

God intended for the Man and the Woman to rule creation on his behalf, but they rebelled against his intentions.

Now he wants Moses to lead the Israelites on his behalf.
God could free the Israelites all by himself with overwhelming display of supernatural power. After all, he really is all-powerful, as he reminds Moses.[13] But central to the heart of God is his desire for people to freely partner with him in his redemptive purposes.[14] God consistently wants to partner with people.

And eventually Moses takes the job.
He'll partner with this God.

---

[12] Ex 3:1-10.
[13] Ex 4:11.
[14] Ex 4:12.

And this God introduces himself
in a brand new way to Moses.

The word "god," after all, can mean a great many things. Every religion
(of both that day and today) has different understandings of what the
word "god" means. For example, Egypt celebrated an entire pantheon of
"gods" with Pharaoh himself supposedly being an embodiment of Horus,
the sun god.[15]

At the burning bush, however, Moses—along with us—gets a lesson
here about who precisely this "god" is.

His name is Yahweh.[16]

This name will later become so sacred to the Israelites that they will
refuse to pronounce it. If they came across this sacred name when
reading out loud, they would substitute another word. Instead of uttering
this name, they would say "Adonai," a title of reverence meaning "my
master" or "my lord."

So over the centuries, the tradition of this substitution made its way into
almost all translations of Scripture. This is why you will almost always
find **"LORD"** (with small capital letters) instead of **"Lord"** (with lower-case
letters) in the Old Testament. Wherever you find LORD, you are not
reading a depersonalized title—despite how centuries of translation may
inadvertently make it seem. You are reading a personal name.

This is not just any "god" or "God."
This the One God.

---

[15] Nahum Sarna, *Exploring Exodus* (New York: Shocken Books, 1986), 105.
[16] Sometimes translated "Jehovah" based on a Latin translation of the Hebrew (and later Greek) texts.
The name actually is a combination of constants with no vowels, YHWH, but we will render it Yahweh for
the sake of reading.

This is not just any "lord" or "Lord."
This is the LORD.

This is Yahweh.

Yahweh explains that he is the God who appeared to Abraham, Isaac and Jacob. He is the all-powerful, unrivaled, good, creating, judging, promise-making, redeeming God of the universe. Moses will rally the Israelites behind this name and this identity.[17] And so Moses heads back to Egypt with only a staff in his hand and this unmatched name of Yahweh on his lips.

In the subsequent chapters of Exodus we find an epic clash of the gods. A dramatic duel unfolds between the gods of Egyptians (represented in Pharaoh) and the God of their slaves (represented in Moses).

Who will show themselves living and able?
Who will prove to be true?
Who has power and who is the sham?

In ten terrifying plagues, Yahweh trounces all the powers and "gods" of Egypt. Almost every resource in Egypt was revered, but Yahweh shows that he commands the animals, the weather, the Nile and even the sun.[18] During these plagues, Yahweh shows himself supreme to Israel while pulverizing Egypt's pride.

But still Pharaoh refuses to release the Israelites. So in a devastating, final plague, Yahweh warns that all of Egypt's firstborn will die at midnight.[19]

---

[17] Ex 3:16-17.
[18] Ex 7:14-12:30.
[19] Ex 11:1-8.

Pharaoh won't release his death-grip on Yahweh's firstborn son[20] and brings divine judgment on every Egyptian firstborn.

But the Israelites will find shelter from this judgment.

Yahweh commands one-year-old lambs without defect to be killed as twilight settles. The Israelites must paint the sides and tops of their doorframes with the blood of these slaughtered lambs:

The blood will be a sign for you on the houses where you are, and when I see the blood, I will pass over you. No destructive plague will touch you when I strike Egypt.[21]

Deliverance is coming very very soon. They're told to eat this lamb quickly during the night. And to go ahead and bake bread, but no yeast— there's just not time for dough to rise. Stay in pajamas or don't even put them on.[22] They're all about to leave skip town; they're leaving Egypt.

This is the first celebration of the Feast of Unleavened Bread, still celebrated right up to our own day.

This is Passover.

Yahweh warned Moses that Pharaoh would refuse to listen.[23] And mysteriously enough, Yahweh also explained how he himself would actually be causing Pharaoh not to listen.[24]

---

20 In Ex 4:22, Israel is referred to as Yahweh's firstborn "Son." This is an incredibly interesting title that the kings of Israel—and eventually Jesus—will inherit.
21 Ex 12:13. (Ex 12:1-30 recounts the entire story.)
22 Ex 12:8-11.
23 Ex 3:19.
24 Ex 4:21.

Pharaoh is hardening himself. And Yahweh is hardening him.[25]

Again uncreated power and human responsibility work together. The Creator's sovereignty and creation's freedom are both reality.

The final plague arrives, and the firstborn of Egypt all perish. Only in this dreadful defeat does Pharaoh finally relinquish his hold on the Israelites. Yahweh proves himself to be alive and powerful and true. The gods of Egypt are exposed as a sham.

Yahweh's firstborn son, Israel, is free to leave Egypt. And the Israelites leave in style, loading up on gold, silver and clothes on their way out.[26] These aren't merely blood-born Israelites, mind you, but all kinds of other ethnic groups.[27] As long as one agreed to be circumcised (the symbol of trusting and submitting to Yahweh), one was free to join the ranks of the redeemed. To celebrate Passover and escape from Egypt's power.[28]

After they have left, Pharaoh almost immediately regrets his decision. With a massive block of his workforce leaving, the soap scum is building in the shower and the pyramids have stopped rising.[29] He's made a huge mistake.

Pharaoh's wounded pride stings too.
The sham exposed means Pharaoh exposed.

He is not a god—not Horus incarnate.
He is just a pitiful, stubborn man.

---

25 Contrast Ex 7:3, 13, 23; 8:15, 19, 32; 9:7, 34 with Ex 9:12; 10:20, 27; 11:10.
26 Ex 12:36, as promised in 3:22b.
27 Ex 12:38.
28 Ex 12:48-49.
29 Ex 14:5.

And now he's been humiliated by these rag-tag slaves and by this "Yahweh." But he can fix this mistake—prepare the chariots!

Pharaoh will prove his power to his people, to his officials and perhaps even to himself. Suddenly the armies of Egypt's armies are tearing across the desert in hot pursuit of the Israelites.[30]

Meanwhile, Yahweh has been leading his people. He's guided them as a pillar of cloud by day and a pillar of fire by night.[31] His path has led across the desert to the edge of the sea. It's time for one final, spectacular act—to rescue the powerless, break the proud and glorify Yahweh. An act that will be retold forever.[32]

Pharaoh's army begins closing in on the Israelites.

The scene becomes chaos and panic: shouting Egyptians, screaming children. Noise and dust from the chariots fill the air. With their backs against the sea, the Israelites moan in despair. This fool Moses has brought them to their deaths.

Moses pleads with Yahweh for guidance. Yahweh replies for Moses to raise his staff and lead the people through the sea.[33] So Moses does...

...And the Israelites went through the sea on dry ground, with a wall of water on their right and on their left.[34]

Like Noah and baby Moses, the Israelites find rescue by passing safely through water. And at just the right moment, Yahweh allows Pharaoh and

---

30 Ex 14:9.
31 Ex 13:20-22.
32 Ex 14:4. And, fitting the Biblical pattern, this final act will work through both Pharaoh's free decision and according to God's own providential plan (Ex 14:5-6 and 14:8).
33 Ex 14:10-18.
34 Ex 14:22.

his army to pursue the Israelites through the sea. But Moses stretches out his staff again, and Yahweh returns the sea to its proper place.

The armies of the world's strongest power are swept away by the God of the Israelites—by the hand of Yahweh.[35]

Even the wind and the waves obey him.

This moment will define Israel's history. This deliverance from the clutches of Egypt will be remembered by countless generations of Israelites in poetry, songs and psalms. Examples of these songs can be found throughout Scripture (especially in the psalms and the prophetic literature). But if you can't wait that long, two examples are recorded immediately afterward: the song of Moses and the song of Miriam:[36]

> "I will sing to the LORD, for he is highly exalted
>> Both horse and driver he has hurled into the sea."[37]

It's difficult to overestimate how powerfully the exodus from Egypt (most notably Passover and the deliverance at the sea) shapes the memory and mindset of Israel.

Israel will forever remember Yahweh as the God who liberates them from oppression.

Yahweh has liberated them, however, for a purpose.

They weren't freed from Egypt to just be any old nation.
They have been freed to become Yahweh's nation.

---

[35] Ex 14:23-31.
[36] Both of these songs are recorded in Exodus 15.
[37] Ex 15:1.

And Yahweh's plan is not just about Israel.
It never was.

God's plan has always been to bless the entire world.

This world now full of Egypts, Babels, Cains, thorns, and serpents.

So the Israelites are following Moses back to the mountain of the burning bush. Following him back to Sinai. They're about to find out exactly what they've been chosen for.

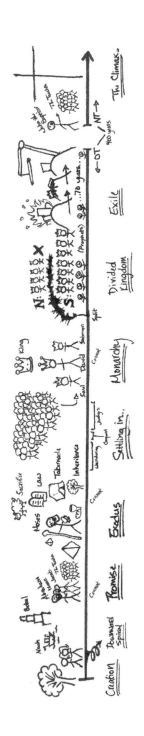

05 elected

Yahweh has redeemed Abraham's descendants from slavery. The God of the slaves has proven himself supreme. Furthermore the gods of Egypt have been shown as a sham. The Israelites depart Egypt in a dramatic exodus, chiefly remembered for the sacrifice of Passover and the deliverance at the sea.

Abraham's family has been chosen—they've been elected—to bless the rebellious ruins of his good creation. They're deep in the wilderness and quickly coming to the very mountain where Yahweh appeared to Moses in a fiery bush.[1]

This mountain called Sinai looms large as they arrive.

They're not in Egypt anymore.

After making camp, the Israelites hear from Yahweh through Moses. They're told to prepare themselves because in three days Yahweh himself is going to descend onto the mountain.[2] The hours pass in preparation and anticipation—what will it look like for Yahweh to draw close to his chosen people?[3]

As promised, Yahweh finally descends onto the mountain.

---

1 Ex 19:1-2. The mountain is sometimes called Horeb (e.g. Ex 3:1, Deut 5:2), other times Sinai (Ex 19:11, 18, 20 and onward), and still other times "the mountain of God" (Ex 4:27, 18:5).
2 Ex 19:10-13.
3 Ex 19:16-19.

God comes down in fire… it's been fifty days since Passover.[4]

Yahweh beckons Moses to the top of this mountain to meet with him.[5]
Filled with delight and filled with dread, the people watch as Moses
climbs the mountain, finally vanishing through the smoke.

The rest of Exodus (along with the entire book of **Leviticus**) details the
instructions Israel receives at the mountain of God. Here Abraham's
family discovers what they've been chosen for:

Yahweh will instruct them how on life—through the law.
Yahweh will assure them of his presence—in the tabernacle.
Yahweh will display his justice and grace—through the sacrifices.

Law, tabernacle, sacrifice.

All three of these gifts will prepare the Israelites for living in the land long-
promised to Abraham. But we can't ever forget why they're inheriting this
land. The land—and every other aspect of Israel's election—is ultimately
for the sake of the world. For that broken world whose wreckage
smolders from Cain to Babel to Egypt and beyond.

Israel is entrusted with the precious promise that there is hope for the
world—that the Creator is recreating and restoring.

The picture of Mount Sinai is often remembered as the place where
Israel receives God's law. But before there's any kind of law, Yahweh
reminds the Israelites the reality of recent history:

---

[4] These "fifty" days between Passover and Sinai will later be translated "Pentecost" in Greek. The
celebration of Pentecost ("Shavuot" in Hebrew) continues to be celebrated to this day.
[5] Ex 19:20.

He has rescued them from Egypt.[6] They didn't earn or merit or achieve that. It was freely given to them. That's the kind of God Yahweh is. The kind of God who rescues all who are willing. Yahweh has rescued them by his grace. Only after grounding them in this grace, does Yahweh offer instruction:

This instruction begins with the "Ten Words."[7]
These are often remembered as "the Ten Commandments."

While these words of instruction do illuminate our personal morality, their original thrust is for shaping community.[8]

Israel is meant to live as a different kind of nation in the world.

As light in the midst of darkness.
As order in the midst of chaos.
As life in the midst of death.

This nation exists for the rest of the nations.

Yahweh describes it this way:

"Now if you obey me fully and keep my covenant, then out of all nations you will be my treasured possession. Although the whole earth is mine, you will be for me a kingdom of priests and a holy nation."[9]

Yahweh is making another "covenant."

---

6 Ex 19:3-4, 20:2.
7 Ex 20:1-17.
8 See Eugene Peterson's helpful, accessible comments in *Christ Plays in Ten Thousand Places* (Grand Rapids: Eerdmans, 2005), 259. In fact, anything that Peterson has written would be great to read.
9 Ex 19:5-6a.

We first heard about "covenants" back when Yahweh made his promises to Abraham. But it's important to distinguish the deal made back with Abraham from the deal made here. These are two separate covenants.

The promises made to Abraham had no stipulations, conditions or fine print.[10] Abraham was going to be blessed with vast family, the land was going to be given to them, and the nations were going to be blessed.

That was a one-sided covenant made by Yahweh.

This covenant here at Sinai, however, has some big stipulations attached to it. Abraham's descendants have responsibilities in this one. And the stipulations are clearly marked—this ain't no fine print hidden from everyone. This thing is two-sided.

They must follow Yahweh's instruction.
They must be a holy kingdom of priests for the sake of the world.

If they don't, they will be thrown out of the land.[11]
If they don't, the Sinai covenant will be broken.

It's important to recognize that the promises to Abraham do not depend on the stipulations of Sinai.

Remember that Yahweh is on the hook with no conditions for his promises to Abraham—he put himself on the hook. The Israelites, on the other hand, share responsibility in this Sinai covenant. They have been redeemed from slavery by God's grace alone, but their possession of the "promised land" is tied up with their obedience.

---

[10] Gen 15 recounts the story of Yahweh making his covenant with Abram. In the story, however, the only person to pass between the halves of sacrificed animals—the cultural sign that you've committed yourself to uphold the deal—is Yahweh. Not Abram.
[11] e.g. Lev 18:24-28, Deut 30:17-18. Leviticus 18 uses the colorful language of the land vomiting the Israelites out, should they rebel, disobey and ignore their calling in the world.

But Yahweh's promise to bless the world through Abraham will always stand. It is *going to happen*. Take it to the bank.

After these first "Ten Commandments," we move into less familiar territory. Yahweh's instruction addresses a wide range of societal, legal and personal situations.[12] His instruction is expansive and comprehensive.

Who hasn't wondered what all these laws were about? Who hasn't flipped through these early biblical books and been bewildered?

Well, the law (or "Torah") serves originally as a sort of governing constitution for the budding nation of Israel. It gives definition, regulation and purpose to their nation in the midst of the Ancient Near East. With some commands, it ensures that Israel will remain distinct from its neighbors.[13] With some rituals, it gives the people's imaginations a framework for understanding what it means for them (as rebellious, death-infected creatures) to be closely interacting with Yahweh (the holy, life-giving Creator).[14] At its core, however, the instruction of Torah is rooted in the Israelites being like their Creator and Redeemer.

Israel is to be holy as Yahweh is holy.[15]
God's people are meant to be like God.

They will be the nation that relearns what it means to love and live like the Creator.[16] They will be a kingdom of priests that embodies and reflects the Creator's image—as all humanity was meant to.

---

12 The law is given initially in Exodus and Leviticus but leaks into parts of Numbers and is retold in Deuteronomy.
13 This is accomplished primarily through Sabbath-keeping, circumcision and the food laws.
14 This can be seen of the purity laws (e.g. Lev 11-15). You would be grateful for this sort of symbolic worldview (capitalizing on cultural taboos), if God lived three tents down from you.
15 Lev 19:2.
16 Deut 6:4-6.

Moses descends from the heights—it's time to seal this covenant between Yahweh and Israel with a formal ceremony. The agreement is read aloud to the people, and the people respond together that they will obey. Sacrifices are made to Yahweh as they prepare for a feast of celebration. Moses stands before the people and sprinkles them with from these sacrifices. He proclaims, *"This is the blood of the covenant that the LORD has made with you in accordance with all these words."*[17]

So the covenant is confirmed.

The Israelites agree to be Yahweh's holy kingdom of priests.

But we don't have to wait long to see humanity's idolatrous heart beating its rebellious rhythm within Israel.

Moses ascends back up the mountain after the feast, this time with his aide Joshua.[18] And he's gone a long time. So the people become impatient—it's widely agreed that Moses has been gone too long. In their restlessness, they persuade Moses' brother, Aaron—who has been a significant leader throughout the entire exodus—to create a god for them to worship.

They bring the gold.
Aaron crafts a calf.

Perhaps this is some kind of new god.
Or maybe it's meant as a representation of Yahweh.[19]

---

17 Ex 24:3-8.
18 Ex 24:13.
19 Ex 32:1-6 . The choice of a calf may very well have been influenced by the various cults in Egypt. But it is difficult to tell whether Israel is trying to have another "god" besides Yahweh or simply putting God into an idolatrous box.

Either way, they were instructed with Ten Words and—in no time flat—have broken either Word One or Word Two.

The people are laughing and dancing, rioting and rebelling.

Aaron is nervous.

Moses and Yahweh are furious.

It's like this covenant has failed before it has begun.[20]

Moses (eventually) defuses the situation by interceding on behalf of the Israelites. He says he himself would rather be destroyed than allow these rebellious people to die.[21] He'd rather substitute himself and die as their representative.

Yahweh doesn't take this brave man up on his offer.

The people were impatient for a visible reminder that the presence of their God—or any god—in their midst.

Sure, they could see, hear and touch Yahweh's agent, Moses. Sure, Yahweh had led them by pillars of fire and cloud. Sure, Yahweh had descended in a blaze onto this mountain. But they want a tangible reminder of his presence that they can see in front of them, that they can carry with them.

And God gives them what they need—the tabernacle.

That's the way God is.

---

20 The events of Ex 32:15-20 are not simply that tablets written by God himself are broken but also give us the first glimpse that a new covenant (Jer 31:31-34) is eventually going to be needed.
21 Ex 32:30-35.

He meets us where we are.

Yahweh instructs them to fashion an incredibly elaborate tent.
A "portable Sinai," if you will.[22]
In that tent, Yahweh will make his presence known among them.

In spite of their rebellion, corruption and idolatry, Yahweh remains a God committed to being with his people.[23]

God gives detailed plans for building this grand tent and the Israelites follow the instructions to the letter.[24] They place the ark of the covenant inside the innermost part of this tent called the "holy of holies." And at at the climactic end of Exodus, God fills this tent with his presence. Yahweh will walk Israel's camp as he walked Eden's garden.[25]

Looking for the all-powerful God of the universe?
He's three tents down.

With one look at this tent, any Israelite can proclaim with bone-shaking fear and heart-stopping joy: "God is with us."

This is good news, but it's also terrifying. The golden calf serves as a screaming reminder that humanity is unholy, rebellious and death-infected. Israel is corrupt like the rest of creation. How can they stand in the blazing, life-giving presence of God? God gives them an answer:

---

22 As termed by Terence Fretheim, *Exodus* (Louisville: John Knox Press, 1991), 294.
23 As clarification, the threat to not go with Israel found in 33:3 is left contingent as seen in 33:5. Indeed, the construction and filling of the tabernacle makes it clear that Yahweh indeed decided to go with Israel.
24 The explaining of the plans covers Ex 25-30 and the actual building spans Ex 36-40.
25 Compare Gen 3:8 and Lev 26:11-12.

The sacrifices.[26]

By these sacrifices, the Israelites can express their devotion to Yahweh and be assured of their standing before him. He even establishes an annual ceremony called the Day of Atonement to assure the Israelites that all of the community's sins are "atoned" for.[27] They can trust that they are "at one" with God again.

The Levites—descendants of Jacob's son Levi—get designated as the "tribe" of Israel responsible for carrying out these sacrifices as well as maintaining the tabernacle.[28] They become the priests within the kingdom of priests.

Israel has been given so much:
the law, the tabernacle, the sacrifices.

Graced with these gifts, the Israelites prepare to leave Mount Sinai and enter into the land promised to Abraham. They are ready to receive their inheritance.

A census of each of the twelve tribes is conducted before they depart, and thus begins the aptly named book of **Numbers**.[29] After the census is completed, the Israelites formally dedicate the tabernacle and celebrate Passover one more time.[30]

Then it's time to go.

---

[26] Lev 1-7 are the primary explanation passages for the four main types of sacrifices: burnt offering, meal offering, peace offering and purification offering. See Part 1 of Allen Ross, *Holiness to the LORD* (Grand Rapids: Baker, 2002) for fuller explanations on each of these. See also pages 129-141 in *Exodus and Leviticus for Everyone* by John Goldingay.

[27] Lev 16.

[28] e.g. Num 1:47-53.

[29] Ex 19:1, Num 1:1.

[30] Num 1-4, Num 6:22-7:89, Num 9:14 respectively.

They have been at Sinai for almost a year.

They begin to follow the guiding presence of Yahweh toward the land.[31]
As they approach the borderlands of Canaan, they send out twelve spies
to scout out both the land and the military situation.[32] After forty days of
exploration, the spies return. Ten of the spies offer an abysmal
assessment. They do indeed think that the land is beautiful, but they also
think its inhabitants are too powerful. This land will never be theirs.

They think Yahweh cannot be trusted.

Only two spies believe that Yahweh can give them the land.[33]
Only two of the twelve trust Yahweh.

Well, this grim majority-report sends waves of rebellion throughout the
community. Moses tries to pacify the mounting uprising, but the people
turn violent against his leadership.[34] Yahweh himself finally has to
intervene, and he's had it with this generation of Israelites. No one in this
generation (except for the two spies) will enter into the promised land.[35]

The land of promise was so close.
But they refused to trust.

We can almost hear Moses now: "Turn around, people! We're going to
wander in this blasted desert for a long time as aimless, homeless
nomads. It's going to do this for a long time—forty years, in fact! A year
for every day the spies were gone.[36] Until your entire generation has died
out! Come on!"

---

31 Num 9:15-23.
32 Num 13:1-25.
33 Num 13:26-33. These two spies are Joshua and a man named Caleb.
34 Num 14:1-10a.
35 Num 14:20-25.
36 Num 14:34.

This brings us to the other way to remember the book of Numbers... as a book about counting... counting people drop dead in the desert.

One by one by one.

Until this entire rebellious, complaining generation has died, not one person will be entering the land.

One dead. Two dead.
Start counting.

Forty incredibly long years pass.

Finally the next generation of Israelites ready themselves.

It's been four decades.

It's time to enter the land.
It's time to trust Yahweh.

These new children of Abraham are preparing themselves just east of the Jordan River and the Dead Sea. [37] They've inherited so much from their parents' generation—the law, the tabernacle, the sacrifices. And now, here they are, on the plains of Moab, finally about to inherit the promised land.

Moses—now ancient with a shock of white hair—gives three speeches to this next generation. These speeches—which comprise the bulk of **Deuteronomy**—remind the people who Yahweh is and who they are.[38]

---

[37] Num 33:48-49.
[38] First speech found in Deut 1:5-4:40. Second speech found in Deut 5:1-26:15. Third speech found in Deut 29:2-30:20.

This new generation has neither grumbled nor rebelled against Yahweh like their parents. But they've also never seen his power displayed firsthand (except, of course, for the manna they've been eating as they wandered the wilderness). So it's important that they never forget the basics:

They need to remember that Yahweh redeemed them from Egypt.[39] And so: *Love the LORD your God with all your heart and with all your soul and with all your strength.*[40]

Moses lays out the two different paths that they (and every coming generation) can choose—obedience or rebellion. Obedience will mean walking in Yahweh's favor and blessing.[41] Disobedience will mean wandering into Yahweh's curse and exile from the land.[42] Obedience will mean life. Disobedience will mean death.

Life and prosperity. Or death and destruction.

Yahweh implores them to choose life.[43]
That's the kind of God he is.

Yet despite his desires for them, we hear an ominous prediction:

One day Israel will, in fact, choose rebellion.

Their corrupt hearts will unravel their nation.
They will fall under the curse of exile.

---

[39] Deut 7:12 is an example of this reminding that is found frequently throughout the Pentateuch (Genesis Exodus, Leviticus, Numbers, Deuteronomy) as well as the rest of the Old Testament.
[40] Deut 6:5.
[41] Deut 28:1-14.
[42] Deut 28:15-68.
[43] Deut 30:15-20.

But Yahweh promises he will eventually renew the covenant. He will gather Israel back to himself and won't be just circumcise the physical bodies of the males. No—in a strange twist of an image, Yahweh will circumcise the hearts of his people so they can truly love him, can truly obey him, and can truly choose life.[44]

That's the kind of God he is.

We've been through quite a bit with Moses, but now his death is close.[45] He announces that his aide, Joshua, will now lead the people and will bring them across the Jordan River into the land.[46] And as the book of Deuteronomy ends, Moses dies on a mountain overlooking the land of Canaan.

The baby from the Nile, called by Yahweh to defy the gods of Egypt and redeem Israel, is gone. The scroll of Deuteronomy ends lamenting how there's never since been prophet like Moses.[47]

But Yahweh promised that one will eventually come.[48]

After a month of grieving, Joshua sets his face eastward. With an excited new generation of Israelites following him, he advances.

Toward the land.
Finally into the land.

These people are going to be a nation.
The Israelites are going to become Israel.

---

44 Deut 30:1-6.
45 Moses' disobedience of Yahweh's command in Num 20:1-13 prevents him from being able to bring Israel into the land.
46 Deut 31:1-8. See also Num 27:12-23.
47 Deut 34:10-12.
48 Deut 18:15-18.

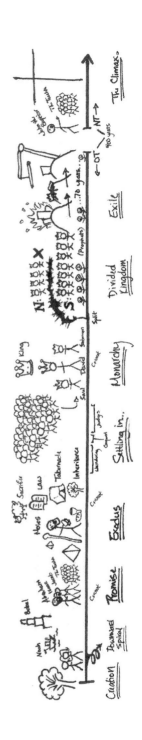

06 settling in

Yahweh rescued the Israelites from slavery for a purpose—they have been "redeemed" for a reason. It's the same reason Abraham was chosen. They're blessed to be a blessing to the world. They're to be a nation of light in a world of darkness.

Yahweh has carried them safely out of Egypt through the sea and into the wilderness of Sinai. They have been entrusted with the law, the tabernacle and the sacrifices. And even though one generation's distrust managed to postpone their inheritance, they're finally ready to receive the land long-promised to Abraham.

The books of Joshua, Judges and Ruth plunge us into this period.

A quick glance ahead:

Joshua will describe the "conquering" and settling of the land.[1] Then Judges will tell stories from the early years in the land when Yahweh (again and again) raised up folksy, charismatic leaders to rescue and reorient the Israelites. And finally, Ruth will shift our attention from this dark period of "the judges" to the hope for of a great, unifying king. That's the shape of things to come, but now back to the son of Nun who has succeeded Moses. He's got some big shoes to fill.

---

[1] I use quotes because Israel is really receiving the land from Yahweh rather than conquering the land by their own strength.

The Israelites march into the land under his new leadership. Their hearts still ache heavily from the death of their beloved Moses. But the sun is rising on their backs as they march westward into the land. A new day is dawning on a new generation. They reach the river Jordan full of excitement and hope, full of trust in both Yahweh and their new leader **Joshua**.[2]

Their trust will not be disappointed.

Joshua stirs distant memories of their parents flight from Egypt as he leads them to the river's shore. Before they know it, they're passing through the Jordan on dry ground in the exact same way their parents did.

But this time they're running *to* something not *from* something.

They're not fleeing in fear.
They're following in faith.

Abraham's children have entered the land of promise.[3] Thus begins what many call "the conquest." This name, however, is rather misleading. If we read the story carefully—taking it seriously on its own terms—Yahweh is *giving* the land to the Israelites. God is fulfilling the promises made to Abraham, Isaac and Jacob.[4]

While Yahweh does indeed give this land by granting them favor in battle, they're no more conquering the land in their own power than Moses conquered the powers of Egypt in his own power. These weary desert-beaten nomads can no more conquer this land than they can fly.

---

2 Josh 1:16-17.
3 Josh 3:1-5:1.
4 Josh 1:6.

As we've seen before, Yahweh works through people to bring about his purposes. With Moses, he redeemed the Israelites from slavery and brought judgment to an arrogant, oppressive world-power. With this generation, he will give them the land of promise and bring judgment on the rampant evil already there.

The Israelites have already engaged in sporadic conflicts throughout the previous two books,[5] but the battles begin in earnest in the book of Joshua.

The first half of Joshua describes the defeat of various people groups and cities.[6] The fall of the city of Jericho (where "the walls came tumbling down") is one of the first and most well-known, but there are plenty of others.[7] There is no shortage of blood, sweat and battle in the book of Joshua's first act.

In the second part of the book, however, Joshua, the Israelites and the land itself find rest from war.[8] The story which had perhaps begun to sound like an excessive battle cry, now turns away from war. Instead it becomes a sonnet of establishing peaceful borders and parcelling out the land.

Let's be clear: the Bible is not ultimately a story about war and violence. The Bible is ultimately about the good but corrupted creation being blessed through Abraham's offspring. The narrator of Joshua wants us to remember that, reminding us again and again how Yahweh has fulfilled one of his promises to Abraham.[9]

---

5 e.g. Num 21:1-3, 21-35; Deut 2:24-3:11.
6 Roughly chapters 1-12 with the second half covering chapters 13-24.
7 The battle of Jericho is recorded in Josh 5:13-6:27. Josh 12:7-24 presents a somewhat swaggering summary of the military campaign.
8 Josh 11:23b, 23:1.
9 Josh 21:43-45, 23:14.

The Israelites are not taking, conquering or stealing this land.

Yahweh is giving it to them.

It is a gift.
It is grace.

Yahweh is working to fulfill his promises
to bring blessing back to his tattered world.

But the consistent message of the Bible is that the work of blessing also
inevitably involves the judgment of evil.

So what are we to make of these battles and wars?

These military stories are some of the hardest for our (modern, Western)
culture to read.[10] After all, stories of Yahweh conquering nations through
the Israelites can appear at first (or fifty-first!) glance to be the backward,
barbaric stories of ancient divinely-endorsed genocide. At worst, they can
be twisted to justify holy wars, militaristic national aggression, or maybe
even economic colonialism today.

These stories are terrific examples of why it's *absolutely essential* to read
these stories of battles within the larger story of Yahweh's redemptive
purposes for the entire world.

To read every part of the Bible in light of the whole of the Bible.

Yahweh is not giving this land to Israel through battle because there is
anything special or good in them. It is actually quite the opposite—the

---

[10] Interestingly, many other cultures today would consider Jesus' commands to love enemies and forgive
freely as embarrassingly weak and shameful.

Israelites are puny and rebellious![11] Rather Yahweh gives this land to them through battle for the dual purposes of fulfilling his promises and judging evil.

Yahweh's loyal love for Abraham compels him to give the land to the Israelites.[12] He remains faithful to his promises—and we need to always remember that his biggest promise is to bless the entire world through them.

The Creator loves his creation with fierce loyalty.[13]

It is God's love for creation
that compels God to judge evil.

And who doesn't want injustice and wickedness dealt with?

Make no mistake, those inhabiting the land are incredibly dark and depraved. These are not people that Yahweh has become a little annoyed with—as if they slept through church or swore when they stubbed their toe. No, these are dangerous, depraved people promoting a dangerous, depraved culture.

The land's inhabitants have become so utterly corrupted that they have embraced dark practices such as bestiality and sacrificing children.[14] And while the corruption of their culture may not make the tough judgment recounted here easier to digest, it at least gives it some context. This culture of injustice is exactly why Yahweh commands the Israelites to totally destroy those in the land.[15] Yahweh as the good Creator who

---

11 Deut 7:7 and Deut 9:6. What a bizarre history this would be for Israel to write about themselves if they were simply making it all up.
12 Deut 7:8.
13 Ps 89:11-15.
14 Lev 18:21-25.
15 Deut 20:16-18.

loves justice *must* stop their evil deeds and *must* stop them from spreading.[16] And so he uses Israel as a scalpel to cut cancer out of his creation.

Yahweh judged with a flood of water in Noah's day.
Yahweh judges with a flood of Israelites in Joshua's day.

Despite the story's sweeping language of annihilation, many of the land's inhabitant's were (evidently) not completely wiped out. We don't have to search hard for an example:

The narrator states boldly: *No Anakites were left in Israelite territory.*[17] Yet a chapter later we find weathered, old Caleb (one of the two spies) claiming his portion of the land and driving Anakites away from it.[18] If they were *literally* all destroyed, there *literally* would not have been any left there.

When we read the Bible closely, we begin to have questions.
And questions are always welcome.

God is big enough to handle these.

He's given us the Bible in this particular, ancient form—instead of some kind of timeless bullet-pointed list of abstract "truths"—and it's quite healthy and necessary to grapple with tensions we might find. When you actually begin to read the text you're going to have to wrestle with the text.

Some theologians consider tensions like this in the text to be ancient figures of speech. One scholar describes it this way: "Just as we might

---

16 Deut 9:4-5.
17 Josh 11:22a.
18 Josh 14:12-15, 15:13-14

say that a sports team 'blew their opponents away' or 'slaughtered' or 'annihilated' them, the author (editor) likewise followed the rhetoric of his day."[19]

This hardly makes the situation any better for those who are struggling with war in the Bible—as if we're all suddenly going to celebrate that the people sacrificing children weren't entirely stopped. It does, however, explain why Israel will so easily fall into these dark practices themselves. They did not wipe them out.

The cancer survived.

By giving the land to the Israelites through battle, Yahweh fulfills his promise to Abraham while simultaneously judging evil.

And all of this for the sake of ultimately blessing his creation.

We must not misread the story—the people of the land are not unloved or rejected outright by Yahweh. That's the point of the story about a woman named Rahab. Anyone willing to become a part of the kingdom of priests and commit their loyalty to Yahweh—even a foreign prostitute and her family—will be grafted into the family of Abraham.[20]

And on the other side of the coin, we must not misread the story—the Israelites are not given a free pass. If you identify yourself with the good, just and holy Yahweh, you must not misrepresent him. Not every Israelite is loyal to Yahweh. Not all want to be holy like Yahweh is holy. That's the point of the story of a crooked Israelite named Achan who is destroyed— along with his family—because of his willful, stubborn disobedience.[21]

---

19 Paul Copan, *Is God a Moral Monster?* (Grand Rapids: BakerBooks, 2011), 171.
20 Josh 2:1-21 and 6:20-25.
21 Josh 7:1-26

The author of Joshua makes these points by putting these two stories—Rahab's rescue and Achan's judgment—back to back.[22] Receiving the land as an inheritance has nothing to do with being a favored ethnic or national group.

God doesn't have a favorite gene pool.
He wants obedient trust.

Those who do, are true "Israelites."
Those who do not, are not.

The Israelites carry the promise of hope that the world will one day be blessed again—that creation will be reconciled back to its good Creator. But if his chosen people become like the rest of the nations, Yahweh continually warns that they will fall under the same just judgment.[23]

So as the book of Joshua ends, the children of Abraham have received the land and are finally settling in. After many years, the land is finally coming under the control of twelve tribes. By now Joshua is very old.[24] He charges the people to follow Yahweh faithfully after his death, and they agree to do just that.[25] Joshua warns them, however, that this is nothing trivial. Yahweh is utterly serious about their task to be a kingdom of priests and a holy nation—he's serious about blessing the world through them.

They need to be absolutely aware of this.
They insist that they are and sign the dotted line.

---

[22] Rahab's story ends in 6:20-25 and Achan's story is told in 7:1-26. It's often enlightening to be aware of larger movements of paragraphs and stories in biblical books (and anything else you're reading) in addition to verses and sentences.
[23] Josh 23:15-16, 24:20. See also Deut 28:15-68.
[24] Josh 23:1.
[25] Josh 24:1-18.

They want to be Yahweh's people.[26]

But it does not take long to recognize what a difficult task actually being Yahweh's people is going to be.

Our own memories are short, and Israel's memory is no different.
Our own hearts are rebellious, and Israel's heart is no different.
Our own wills are stubborn, and Israel's will is no different.

Israel was not chosen because they were exceptional.
They were chosen because they are good examples of us all.

They have an incredibly difficult time obeying Yahweh.

Welcome to the book of **Judges**.

Picking up right where Joshua leaves off, Judges finds the Israelites enjoying their newly "conquered" land. They are not, however, wiping out the dangerous and depraved cultures ingrained in the land.[27]

They're actually beginning to imitate them.

One generation gives way to the next, and the twelve tribes begin serving the gods of their neighbors. This means practicing exactly what Yahweh had forbidden. So Yahweh hands them over into the clutches of their enemies, and they begin to be conquered. They panic and cry out to Yahweh. So Yahweh raises up judges (which could also be translated "leaders") who rescue them from these oppressors. But once they are rescued, they become corrupt and rebellious all over again.

---

26 Josh 24:19-24.
27 See Judg 1.

Repeat the cycle.
Given over, panic, a judge rises, rescue, apathy, corruption.

Repeat the cycle.
This is the pattern of the book of Judges.

And each generation becomes more and more corrupt.[28]

Despite their title, these charismatic leaders of Israel do not wear black robes or have powder-white wigs. They are an eclectic group of men (and women!) ranging from Ehud the assassin[29] and Deborah the commander,[30] to timid Gideon who nobly refuses to be made king and strong Samson who falls to foreign seduction.[31]

Israel repeats its rebellion over and over as Yahweh continues to sends rescuers. By the end of Judges, we are worn out. Why won't these people just obey Yahweh and break this horrible cycle? And as the book comes to a close, we hear a particular refrain repeated four separate times:

In those days Israel had no king.
Each man did what he considered to be right.[32]
The downward spiral that we saw in Genesis 3-11 begins to show the extent of its reach here—how it even infects Yahweh's chosen people. The closing chapters of Judges recount in gruesome detail the sort of dark events happening in the midst of Yahweh's chosen people:

---

28 A concise opening summary of the book of Judges within itself can be found in 2:10-19.
29 Judg 3:12-30.
30 Judg 4:1-24.
31 Judg 6:1-8:35.
32 Judg 17:6.

One tribe (descendants of Jacob's son Dan) commission an idol to be made for them, and then—with that idol at their helm—proceed to annihilate a peaceful, unsuspecting group of people.[33]

In those days Israel had no king.[34]

In another incident, a woman is gang-raped, killed and cut into pieces. Her body parts are then mailed to the rest of the tribes as a way of trying to rally support for justice. And, yes, everyone seeing this is as shocked and appalled as we are.[35]

In those days Israel had no king.[36]

The other tribes decide to punish the perpetrators of this crime, but the Benjamites (descendants of—you guessed it—Benjamin) actually side with the guilty.[37] And so the eleven other tribes attack one of their own. They nearly exterminate the Benjamites.[38] Then, in order to provide this tribe with wives and ultimately babies, the eleven tribes advocate the kidnapping and forced marriage of some local women.[39]

In those days Israel had no king.
Each man did what he considered to be right.[40]

Civil war in the holy nation.
Mutiny in the kingdom of priests.

Dark days have indeed fallen on the family of Abraham.

---

33 Judg 17:1-18:31 (see 18:27).
34 Judg 18:1.
35 Judg 19:1-30 (see 19:30).
36 Judg 19:1.
37 Judg 20:1-16.
38 Judg 20:17-48.
39 Judg 21:1-24.
40 Judg 21:25.

When will the life-giving reign of Yahweh be obeyed?

Yahweh is not king in Israel…
in fact, nobody is.

In the days when the judges ruled, there was a famine in the land.[41]

These are the opening words of the book of **Ruth**. It pierces into the middle of this dark time as a ray of hope. The opening words mention the lack of food, but there is an obvious lack of almost everything needed to sustain life.

It's a famine of food, justice, obedience, goodness, and love.

It's a famine of the rule and reign of the good Creator.

And now we read the story of Ruth, a Moabite woman who becomes a part of the community of Israel. This story takes on incredible significance when we realize that Moabites had been explicitly excluded from the community of Israel by Moses.[42] The Moabites have been trouble for the Israelites in the past—with Moabite women specifically having had a history of leading Israelite men astray.[43]

It's right there in the law: "No Moabites."

Getting too cozy with these "outsiders" is exactly what's been causing such a mess for Israel, isn't it? And yet here we find a Moabite being adopted into the family of Abraham, embodying the loyal love of Yahweh, and bringing hope.

---

[41] Ruth 1:1.
[42] Deut 23:3.
[43] Num 25:1-3.

Evidently even a Moabite woman
can become one of Yahweh's people.

Evidently anyone from anywhere
can become one of Yahweh's people.

But the book of Ruth does more than simply challenge ethnic and
nationalistic assumptions about who can be Yahweh's people. We find
the book of Ruth pointing us toward something bigger when we
remember the closing refrain of Judges:

During the days when the judges ruled, there was a famine in the land...
In those days Israel had no king....

Well, the book of Ruth ends with a genealogy.
Everyone's favorite part of the Bible, right?

Genealogies are actually incredibly interesting. They function as wide-
angle lenses, connecting the dots for us, and letting us know where
these Israelites—where this family of Abraham, where these sons of
Adam—are headed.

This genealogy is a prime example.

The Israelites—who started out with such a high hopes—have spiraled
downward like the wider world around them. Those meant to be a
blessing are becoming part of the problem.

But not everything is lost.

Or maybe everything is lost and the glorious story of the Bible tells us
that God finds, redeems, and rescues that which is lost.

The light of hope bursts through the darkened clouds as we discover that from the family of Ruth (a Moabite, of all things!) will come a king whose name is David.[44]

There will finally be a king in the land.

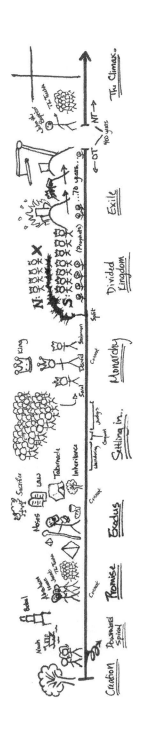

Creation

Downward
Spiral

Promise

Exodus

Settling in...

Monarchy

Divided
Kingdom

Exile

The Climax.

07 monarchy

Yahweh chose to bless the world through Abraham's family, but it began spiraling downward itself. Their early hopes are slowing eroding with generation after generation of Israelites turning from Yahweh despite his repeated rescue. And now their hearts have become so distant that their confederation of tribes is falling apart at the seams.

What will become of the Abraham's family?

Will the holy nation tear itself apart?
Will the bearers of blessing be overtaken by the curse?

Will Yahweh's promise to bless the world fail?

But Yahweh doesn't seem concerned about failing.
In fact, he's about to raise the stakes royally.

During the reign of the judges, a boy by the name of **Samuel** is born. Like Isaac and Jacob before him, Samuel is a child of Yahweh's grace — given to parents who could not conceive.[1] So his very existence confirms that Yahweh answers prayers. And his mother expresses her gratitude by dedicating him back to Yahweh.

---

1 1 Sam 1:1-20.

Samuel's mother places him into the care and service of a priest named Eli.[2] We may remember that the tribe of the Levites are in charge of the tabernacle and the sacrifices. They serve as priests in the service of Yahweh. Well, Eli serves as the priest at Shiloh,[3] an important meeting place for sacred gatherings and corporate worship.[4] Since Eli serves as the priest of such a highly significant location, he is probably functioning as the high priest.[5] That is, he's the chief connection between Yahweh and the Israelites. And more than just that, Eli also functions politically as a "judge" (or "leader") of the people.[6]

Eli is quite the significant figure—religiously and politically.

But Eli's sons are absolutely corrupt.[7] This prominent priestly family reflects the corrupt period. Those who should be upright and holy are actually crooked and despicable. The family at the religious and political heart of Israel has begun to fester and stink—just like the people as a whole.

Samuel is dedicated into the service of this kind of leadership.

And in case you were wondering:
In those days the word of the LORD was rare.[8]

So you can imagine young Samuel's surprise when one night Yahweh speaks to him.

The word of Yahweh! Finally!

---

[2] 1 Sam 1:25-28, 2:11.
[3] 1 Sam 1:9.
[4] Josh 18:1 and Judg 18:31.
[5] David Freedman, ed., *The Anchor Bible Dictionary* vol 2 (New York: Doubleday, 1992), s.v. "Eli" (by Ronald Youngblood).
[6] 1 Sam 4:18b.
[7] 1 Sam 2:12.
[8] 1 Sam 3:1a.

What kind of life-giving words will Yahweh speak?

"Blessing is coming on the other side of judgment."

Yahweh tells Samuel that he is going to bring the legacy of both Eli and his family to an end. Judgment is about to fall on them.[9]

Perhaps Eli preferred the word of the Lord staying away.

True to his word, Yahweh's judgment falls swiftly.

A furious battle brings an end to Eli's sons.
A fumble over a chair sends Eli to join them.[10]

The void of leadership created by their deaths eventually allows Samuel to rise and become the last judge of Israel.[11]

As a judge, Samuel does what so many of the leaders before him have done: he drives back the latest enemies that are threatening Israel—a group called the Philistines. And his leadership allows for a few blessed years of peace.[12]

In addition to defending the people from enemies as a judge, Samuel also serves double-duty as a prophet of Yahweh.[13]

Now we need to immediately clear up a common misconception. The word "prophet" may evoke images of misty-eyed, detached figures gazing into the future. That is not, however, what prophets in the Bible

---

[9] 1 Sam 3:1-18.
[10] 1 Sam 4:1-18.
[11] 1 Sam 7:6b, 7:15.
[12] 1 Sam 7:13-14.
[13] 1 Sam 3:20.

look like. Prophets in Scripture are earthy, grounded people that serve as the messengers of Yahweh. They speak his word. Sometimes this may indeed involve speaking *about* the future, but more often it involves speaking *into* the present:

What should the reign of Yahweh look like in the present?

Again, Yahweh's word for the present may sometimes talk about the future but this is not the primary interest of a prophet.

Prophets are not fortune-tellers.

We'll be getting better acquainted with prophets in chapter eight, but right now we're going to see Samuel embody one of the most important functions of a prophet:

He is going to anoint a king for Israel.

Anointing a king, however, was not really what Samuel wanted. He really wanted his sons to follow in his footsteps and rule over Israel as judges. Unfortunately, when he finally appoints them to leadership, Samuel's sons wind up being as corrupt as Eli's.

And the people demand a king.[14]

The conflict compounds further because Samuel recognizes the people's primary motive for wanting a king is not pure. They want a king so that they can be *similar to* the nations around them instead of *different from* them.[15]

---

[14] 1 Sam 8:1-5.
[15] 1 Sam 8:5.

Israel was, of course, created to be a kingdom of priests under the kingship of Yahweh. But now they want to be a kingdom like all others under the kingship of a common man.

What should Samuel do?

Their motives run opposite to their calling.

Yahweh comforts Samuel by telling him to grant their demand: *"Listen to all that the people are saying to you; it is not you they have rejected, but they have rejected me as their king. As they have done from the day I brought them up out of Egypt until this day, forsaking me and serving other gods, so they are doing to you."*[16]

Both Yahweh and Samuel warn Israel that a human king will make all kinds of terrible demands of them. The monarchy won't be as wonderful as they think. But the people insist.[17]

So Samuel anoints a king for Israel.
That king's name is Saul.[18]

Imagine Hugh Jackman.
You've got a good picture.

Saul looks and acts just like they want a king to look and act. He is handsome and tall.[19] He is energetic and charismatic.[20] He is the sort of chap everyone wants to be king. He's the kind of guy you would think

---

[16] 1 Sam 8:7.
[17] 1 Sam 8:9-22.
[18] Saul is anointed as king 1 Sam 9:1-10:8 and actually made king in 10:9-26.
[19] 1 Sam 9:1-2.
[20] 1 Sam 10:9-11.

might finally unite these bickering, conflicted tribes of Israel into one united nation.[21]

And you would be right.

Saul does just that, creating a unified kingdom out of the confederacy. The tribes become a nation—Israel. He also begins dealing with the troublesome neighboring Philistines, just as Yahweh promised he would.[22]

And he looked good doing it all.

Kings in the Ancient Near East were representatives.

Representatives of their people to the gods,
and representatives of the gods to their people.

But as things progress, Saul's kingship develops into a disaster. Saul steps out from among the people and embodies not only their deepest problems. And the chief problem leads to his eventual downfall—Saul willfully and repeatedly refuses to submit himself to Yahweh's rule.

Yahweh wants to reign over the world through Israel. And Yahweh is always looking to partner freely with humanity in doing this. Yahweh's looking for humble servant of a king. But Saul refuses to be that. So eventually Yahweh rejects Saul as king.[23]

Samuel tells Saul: "*You have not kept the command the LORD your God gave you; if you had, he would have established your kingdom over Israel for all time. But now your kingdom will not endure; the LORD has*

---

[21] 1 Sam 10:17-27.
[22] 1 Sam 9:15-16.
[23] 1 Sam 13:6-14, 15:13-23.

sought out a man after his own heart and appointed him ruler of his people, because you have not kept the LORD's command."[24]

So Yahweh leads Samuel to anoint another as king: "a man after Yahweh's own heart."

Well, calling him a man might be a bit of an overstatement.

He's young.
Very young.

Just a kid actually.

Not what you would expect a king to look like.
...I mean, he's no Saul.

Yahweh directs Samuel to the backwater town of Bethlehem to a man named Jesse's house. He must overlook seven older brothers who appear far better qualified to lead the people. But none of that matters to Yahweh: *"People look at the outward appearance, but the LORD looks at the heart."*[25] So Samuel summons the youngest son to be brought in from shepherding in the field.

Like Jacob over Esau, Yahweh now goes against all conventional and cultural wisdom. He chooses Jesse's youngest son.

The youngest will be king.
The least will be the greatest.

---

[24] 1 Sam 13:13b-14.
[25] 1 Sam 16:7b.

Samuel anoints David, son of Jesse from the tribe of Judah from the town of Bethlehem, to be king of Israel.[26]
David has been anointed.

He has been smeared with oil.
He has become "the messiah."[27]

And now... the tension of a world with two kings.

David has been anointed the true king, but Saul is still on the throne. There is an overlapping of monarchies here—a period of waiting for the true king's reign to be revealed. There is a time of "already" but also "not yet." The kingdom of David is certainly here—he's been chosen by Yahweh and anointed by Samuel for crying out loud. But his kingdom is also coming—the day when everyone will know that he is king.

Although David comes from humble origins, his story becomes one of the grandest in the Bible. Unfortunately the scope of our book only allows us the briefest glimpse at his sprawling and epic life. We can only mention in passing how he is enlists into the service of king Saul,[28] defeats a gigantic Philistine champion from Gath[29] and narrowly escapes two assassination attempts by Saul himself.[30] We're only allowed only a brief mention of his intimate friendship with Saul's son,[31] how he sought asylum in hostile territory (Gath, actually) by acting insane[32] and how he nobly spares Saul's life twice.[33]

---

26 1 Sam 16:13.
27 *Messiah* is simply the English transliteration of the Hebrew (MASIAH) meaning "Anointed One." The word translated into Greek is *Christos*. More on this later.
28 1 Sam 16:14-23.
29 One, Goliath by name: 1 Sam 17.
30 1 Sam 18:10-11, 19:9-10.
31 1 Sam 20.
32 1 Sam 21:10-15.
33 1 Sam 24, 26.

All that and more
before he ever even takes
the throne of Israel.

Finally Saul dies in battle along with his son, David's dear friend.[34]

David is devastated. This tragedy is absolutely not the way he had envisioned ascending to the throne, and he grieves deeply for both Saul and Saul's son.[35]

Being from the tribe of Judah, David initially assumes the throne over only that one tribe,[36] but eventually he manages to unite all twelve tribes under his kingship.[37] And with that, the tribes are finally united under a king who is obedient to Yahweh.

A servant king.

David succeeds in conquering a city called Jerusalem and making it his capital.[38] As he settles in, he makes plans to build a temple for Yahweh there.[39] Yahweh, however, has a different idea.

A bigger idea.

You see, while David is wanting to build a house for Yahweh, Yahweh is planning on building a "house" for David: *"The LORD declares to you that the LORD himself will establish a house for you: When your days are over and you rest with your ancestors, I will raise up your offspring to succeed you, your own flesh and blood, and I will establish his kingdom. He is the*

---

34 1 Sam 31.
35 2 Sam 1:17-27.
36 2 Sam 2:1-7.
37 2 Sam 5:1-4.
38 2 Sam 5:6-10.
39 2 Sam 7:1-2, 27.

one who will build a house for my Name, and I will establish the throne of his kingdom forever.[40]

Yahweh is now making a covenant with David. Like he did centuries before with Abraham, Yahweh is making sweeping promises concerning unborn generations.

Yahweh isn't worried about his promises going unfulfilled.
He's making more. He's raising the stakes.

Honestly—the royal line of David will go on forever?

A never-ending kingdom?
This is really big.

And Israel will wrestle with the meaning and implications of these promises about "a king" and "a kingdom" for centuries.

Of course, David's story is by no means all sunshine and rainbows. Israel's account of its great king is surprisingly transparent about his flaws, faults and embarrassments. And there are oh so many. In fact, the remainder of David's life is saturated by suffering and shame—much of it self-inflicted. And we can mark the beginning of this dark turn with the story about an infamous affair with a woman named Bathsheba.

In a nutshell, David uses his kingly position to have sex with the wife of one of his soldiers—a solider presently on the battlefield fighting for David. When she becomes pregnant, David hastily attempts a cover-up. And when the cover-up fails he decides to murder her husband to try to save face.[41]

---

[40] 2 Sam 7:11b-13.
[41] David's affair with Bathsheba is recorded in 2 Sam 11.

Yahweh is not pleased with this at all. Although Yahweh forgives him, David's actions here end up haunting him for the rest of his life. In fact, his life seems to spiral out of control from here on:

The baby born of the scandalous affair dies.[42]

One of David's sons rapes one of David's daughters.[43]

Then the rapist is killed by another of David's sons, Absalom.[44]

Then Absalom overthrows his father's kingship for a time.[45]

Hardly sunshine and rainbows.

Incestual rape and fraternal murder within the royal family.
The son of the king conspiring to overthrow the crown.

This everlasting kingdom is off to a rocky start.

It is during this time that the **Psalms** begin to emerge, many written by David himself. These are songs, poems and prayers expressing everything from overwhelming thankfulness to the deepest levels of anguish—often right next to each other.[46] These psalms show that a God-honoring life of obedient trust does not involve moral spotlessness but rather brutal honesty and painful humility in the midst of our mess.

David understands deep-rooted joy and soul-crushing despair.

And he prays and repents and trusts through it all.

---

[42] 2 Sam 12:13-25.
[43] 2 Sam 13:1-22.
[44] 2 Sam 13:23-28.
[45] 2 Sam 15-18.
[46] Many more will later be written and gathered together over centuries into the collection we now have.

As the darkness of corrupted creation looms heavy over David's life, the promises of Yahweh become more suspenseful:

Blessing the world through Abraham?
Everlasting kingdom through David?

How will all this work out?

Everyone we meet in this story seems incapable of handling their own lives, much less saving the world. The man after Yahweh's own heart shows that wickedness lurks deep even within his heart. If there is to be light that finally banishes this darkness, it will have be from Yahweh himself.

And the great king David eventually dies like everyone else.

He leaves his throne to his son, Solomon.[47]

As Solomon becomes king, Yahweh asks him what he desires, because he can have it. Whatever he would like—just say it. Solomon asks for wisdom.[48] And perhaps asking for wisdom is itself a wise move, because Yahweh gives him not only wisdom but also wealth and honor to such a degree that he will have no equal in his lifetime.[49]

In fact, the only thing that rivals Solomon's wisdom and wealth is his ambition. David had planned to build a temple for Yahweh in Jerusalem

---

[47] 1 Kings 2:12. Solomon's assumption of the throne is not uncontested, and his older brother Adonijah holds the throne briefly in 1 Kings 1.

[48] Many of the **Proverbs** (which provide general guidance about how to live) in the Bible are credited to Solomon. The books of **Ecclesiastes** (which wrestles with the briefness and futility of life) and **Song of Songs** (which celebrates committed, erotic love between two lovers) have also traditionally been ascribed to him.

[49] 1 Kings 3:12-13.

but was prevented by struggles, war and battle. But Solomon builds what his father could not.[50]

He builds a house for Yahweh on Mount Zion in Jerusalem.
The tabernacle becomes the temple.

Just as it once filled the tabernacle, now the glorious presence of Yahweh fills this building.[51]

Solomon spares no expense as he builds the temple over the course of seven years.[52] He fills it with lavish and ornate detail. Furthermore he spends an additional six years working on a grand palace for himself.[53] (After all, why should Yahweh be the only one living in luxury?)

With Solomon's temple and palace complete, the skyline of Jerusalem sparkles brilliantly on the horizon. The nation of Israel enters its "golden age" as far as human eyes are concerned. The Israelites rejoice in their peace and prosperity. Foreign dignitaries leave overwhelmed, shocked and thrilled at the splendor of Jerusalem under Solomon.[54]

And ruling over it all is the son of David.

There sits the gleaming city of Jerusalem, sparkling on a hill.

The kingdom is united.
The people are prosperous.

---

50 1 Kings 5:3-5, 8:17-18, 1 Chr 22:7-9.
51 1 Kings 8:10-11 (compare with the climatic ending found in Ex 40:34-35).
52 1 Kings 6.
53 1 Kings 7:1-12. Notice the transition between 6:38 and 7:1—the Bible is very elegant and subtle in the way it makes its points. We're about to see that Solomon's preoccupation with himself gets everyone in trouble..
54 1 Kings 10:4.

The treasury is full.
Spirits are high.

Things are finally looking up for Israel.

Take a deep breath, savor the view, and soak it all in...
...because things are about to fall apart.

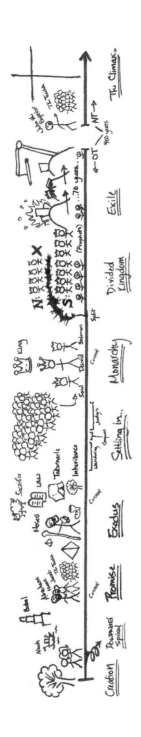

08 divided kingdom

Israel has finally begun to taste "good times." The brilliant sunrise of the monarchy has pierced the darkness of the judges. After a rough start with Saul, the tribes were united as a nation under the rule of David, Yahweh's servant king. And Yahweh made a promise to this king—flawed though he was—that an everlasting kingdom would come from his family.

And perhaps that promise is easier to believe than ever—the son of David, Solomon, sits on the throne, and Jerusalem is gleaming like a jewel under the eastern sun.

Is this the moment when Yahweh will bless the world?

Has the Creator/Judge/Promise-Maker/Redeemer finally shown his cards? Is he unfurling the plan to bring his corrupt, rebellious creation back under his rule and reign?

By many standards, it looks like Abraham's family is making progress. Israel and her king are finally impressing and influencing the nations. How much more ready and positioned could they be to bless the world? Perhaps now, the promise to Abraham will be fulfilled through the never-ending dynasty of David's family. The line of David will march ever forward, climbing ever higher, getting ever better, obeying Yahweh and blessing the world. And they all live happily ever after.

Except that's not the way the story goes.

This nation Solomon rules over, this nation called Israel, was always meant to be different. It never existed to compete against all the other nations for the same things. It was meant to play by different rules—it was meant to show the world what Yahweh intended humanity to be.

Visitors from other nations could even recognize some sort of difference. A visiting foreign queen, for example, can understand Israel's purpose in the world:

"Because of the LORD's eternal love for Israel, he has made you king to maintain justice and righteousness."[1]

The dark irony, however, is that Solomon maintains neither. Because in the later years of his reign, Solomon sets the nation on a path of disastrous disobedience:

He hoards immeasurable riches for himself.[2]
He builds the temple and his palace on the backs of slaves.[3]

He collects horses and chariots, importing them from Egypt and then exporting them to neighboring areas.[4]

(And since these are the tanks and hummers of the day, we should not miss the point that Solomon has become an "international arms dealer."[5])

---

[1] 1 Kings 10:9b.
[2] 1 Kings 10:14-25.
[3] 1 Kings 5:13-18, 9:15-22.
[4] 1 Kings 10:26-29.
[5] Thanks to Walter Brueggemann for this phrase: *Solomon: Israel's ironic icon of human achievement* (Columbia, USC Press, 2005), 125.

He marries hundreds of foreign wives who turn his heart away from Yahweh and lead Solomon to sacrifice to foreign gods.[6]

(This may sound trivial, but it becomes more sinister when we realize that these foreign gods frequently demanded infants as sacrifice.[7] Knowing the darkness of these cultures, Yahweh had strictly forbidden both idolatry[8] and child sacrifice.[9] But Solomon begins practicing—and worse, leading Israel to practice—both.)

Instead of blessing the world, Israel is joining its problems.

The once-oppressed are becoming the oppressors.

Israel is becoming Egypt.
The son of David is becoming Pharaoh.

The kingdom of priests has begun building Babel's tower.
The scalpel has become the cancer that must be cut out.

Yahweh is not pleased with Solomon. Not one bit.

In fact, he promises that he will tear most of the kingdom away from Solomon's son.[10] David's grandson, the next "son of David," will reign over only two tribes. The other ten tribes are going to rebel against the line of David and form another kingdom.[11]

So Yahweh tears the nation apart in judgment. From this point forward there will be two kingdoms, one in the North and one in the South. This needs a little explaining:

---

6 The gods mentioned in 1 Kings 11:4-8 are Ashtoreth and Molech.
7 2 Kings 23:10; Jer 32:35.
8 e.g. Ex 20:4, Lev 19:4, Deut 5:8.
9 Gen 22:12, Lev 18:21, 20:2-5.
10 1 Kings 11:9-13.
11 1 Kings 12:16-24.

These two kingdoms have different names, different kings and different capitals. The **northern kingdom** is comprised of the ten tribes that rebelled. They continue to be known as the kingdom of **Israel**. (If you've got the majority of the tribes, you get to keep the original name, I suppose.)

The smaller, **southern kingdom** consists of the two remaining tribes (Judah and Benjamin). The southern kingdom ruled by David's bloodline becomes known as the kingdom of **Judah**, taking their name from David's tribe.

Judah in the south keeps Jerusalem as its capital, while Israel in the north establishes a new capital city called Samaria.[12]

Solomon dies, Yahweh's judgment falls, the kingdom splits.

At this point, the scope of the biblical story expands. The camera zooms out again, covering miles and centuries much more quickly. The book of **Kings**[13] ricochets back and forth between the ever-changing kings of Israel and Judah.[14] Each king's story is told in only a handful of verses (with a few notable exceptions[15]).

Both kingdoms—Israel and Judah—continue to stubbornly slide down the tragic path of rebellion. Israel's kings are entirely corrupt, leading their people consistently in idolatry. In fact, their first king ironically sets up two golden calves in different locations so that people can better

---

[12] 1 Kings 16:23-24.

[13] Though separated in our Bibles, 1 Kings and 2 Kings (like the books of Samuel and Chronicles too) were originally one large work.

[14] The distinction between these is tough at first. Especially since the story of "Israel" really follows the kingdom of Judah from here on.

[15] One notable exceptions includes 1 Kings 17:1 — 2 King 13:21. These are stories of the prophets Elijah and Elisha, along with the nefarious northern kingdom's King Ahab and his queen, Jezebel. Also noteworthy are the reforms of the southern king, Josiah (2 Kings 22:1-23:30).

worship![16] The kings of Judah are a tiny bit better, with David's descendants occasionally shining light into the darkness. But as a whole, both kingdoms slide into rebellion against Yahweh.

Two kingdoms.
Two sets of kings.
Two nations of rebels.

As the camera zooms out, as time speeds up and as the names of kings quickly change, it's easy to get disoriented in the book of Kings. It's easy to lose perspective on the bigger story. So to help anchor ourselves, we're going to focus our attention on two other influential groups from this time period. Two groups with which the kings of Israel and Judah frequently interact.

One group is personal, the other political.
One a voice of warning, the other a looming threat.

We're talking about the prophets and the empires.

First, the prophets. The prophets really begin stepping into the spotlight during this divided kingdom. Figures like Elijah and Elisha, Hosea and Amos, Isaiah and Jeremiah—they speak out on behalf of Yahweh. Some of these prophets' words are written down and comprise part of the Old Testament.

(Although they are placed after the "wisdom literature" in our Christian Bible,[17] it's very helpful to remember that the prophets who sit near the back of the Old Testament actually overlap with the period of the divided kingdom and Israel's subsequent exile and return.)

---

[16] 1 Kings 12:25-33.
[17] The Hebrew Bible traditionally understood (and still understands) the books of Joshua — Kings to also be "Prophets." It places Isaiah, Jeremiah, and the rest immediately afterward.

One point from an earlier chapter bears repeating because it can cause us a lot of confusion if we forget it:

Prophets are not fortune-tellers.

Prophets are messengers of Yahweh speaking *into* the present, not preoccupied with the future. Speaking into the present often involves speaking against the politics, religious establishment and popular culture of the day. They shouldn't be confused with priests who work and maintain the temple and sacrifices. They are often outsiders to the political/religious system.[18] In fact, very often they are scandalously speaking out against the priests, the temple and the sacrifices.[19]

When "the word of Yahweh" comes to a prophet, they must speak and act. They remind people what the rule and reign of Yahweh ought to look like. This sometimes means anointing kings for Yahweh.[20] Other times a prophet speaks out against the king, against the priests and against the nations—against anyone opposing the goodness and justice of Yahweh. They point their finger at rebellion, idolatry and injustice wherever they see it, whether in paganism or religion. They implore great and small to live in obedience to Yahweh.

To choose life.

Prophets serve as the megaphones of Yahweh.

How exactly they go about this task varies widely from prophet to prophet. Elijah and Elisha spit in the faces of tyrants and perform various

---

18 Other "prophets" appear periodically, such as 1 Kings 22:1-28, where they function in an official vocational capacity. "Prophets" have long been available for hire, such as Balaam in Num 22-24, because—like today—religion can be big business.
19 See Isa 1:10-25, Jer 7:1-11, Amos 5:21-27, Micah 3:9-12 for examples of this.
20 1 Sam 10:1, 16:13; 1 Kings 1:34, 19:15-16.

miracles.[21] Isaiah maintains a working relationship with at least one of the "good kings" of Judah.[22] Jeremiah and Ezekiel, who were both trained as priests, used finely-crafted words and shocking street theater.[23] But they all speak the word of Yahweh into the present, despite their different contexts, techniques, audiences and emphases.

During the time of the divided kingdom, much of what the prophets proclaim is foreboding and frightening. But the word of God is not always gloom and doom; God always speaks what is needed. The prophets will later proclaim hope when hope is needed. But during this glitzy, decadent, rebellious period, they warn:

"Turn back to Yahweh!"
"He will surely—rightfully!—bring judgment on us!"
"We're choosing death! We must choose life!"

Now to the empires. These are other great nations that are conquering and expanding their influence, culture and control. Over the course of world history, various empires have risen and fallen. (The arguably most famous of these, the Roman Empire, is still seven centuries away.)

From the perspective of these empires, both Israel and Judah are small, flea-like nations on their way to Egypt—the rich and fertile "breadbasket" of the ancient world.

From the perspective of Yahweh, however, all of these expansive empires are small, flea-like pawns that he will use to discipline his rebellious people.[24]

---

21 e.g. 1 Kings 17:7-24, 18:16-40; 2 Kings 4:1-7, 42-44; 5:10-14.
22 2 Kings 18-20.
23 e.g. Jer 19, Ezk 4-5. (Of course other prophets did similar things. Like naked Isaiah in Isa 20.)
24 2 Kings 17:5-8, 24:1-4.

The Israelites cannot even recognize how rebellious they have become. They honestly think they doing just fine, thank you very much; much better than all those nasty people in the rest of the world. And in their rebellion, they despise the world rather than bless it.

A prophet named **Jonah** will serve nicely as an example. Yahweh sends him to Nineveh (the capital of an empire called Assyria) because Yahweh wants its citizens to turn away from their evil. Jonah, on the other hand, absolutely refuses to do it. Perhaps you've heard the story of him changing his mind? Eventually he does proclaim to them, and the Assyrian people turn from their evil. They're spared judgment. And this causes Jonah to lash out at Yahweh:

"I knew that you are a gracious and compassionate God, slow to anger and abounding in love, a God who relents from sending calamity."[25]

Yahweh's arms are wide open.
Even to those people on the "outside."

And this makes many Israelites angry. After all, they're Yahweh's chosen people—despite their chronic disobedience. They've lost sight of the fact that Yahweh chose to be *for* the nations, not *above* the nations.

They cannot recognize how wildly off-base they are.

And so Yahweh uses expanding pagan empires to bring judgment on his stubborn, arrogant people. And the first one he'll use will, in fact, be the Assyrian Empire.

Yahweh uses Assyria as his tool for judging the consistently wicked northern kingdom. The kingdom of Israel received plenty of warnings.

---

[25] Jonah 4:2b.

Yahweh had warned that it had chosen a path of destruction as early as its first king (who set up its dual golden calves).[26] More recently, prophets like **Amos** and **Hosea** gave grave warnings against idolatry and social injustice—sure signs that Israel was not not living as humanity was meant to. And finally here in the year 720BC, Assyrian forces march into the northern kingdom and decimate its capital, Samaria.

The Assyrians exile the ten tribes from their land and import various other people groups to resettle their land.[27]

The kingdom formerly known as Israel is gone.

The ten tribes are scattered to the wind.
Only two tribes are left—Benjamin and Judah.

Although Assyria threatens to press further south and take Jerusalem, Yahweh spares that city for the sake of David.[28]

A descendant of David, after all, still sits on Judah's throne.

Yahweh continues sparing the southern kingdom for almost 150 years, and they even manage some reform and repentance.[29] But eventually their rebellion compels Yahweh to bring judgment upon them as well.

By now, the Assyrian empire has been conquered,[30] and another empire named Babylon has risen. Yahweh uses this empire to bring judgment onto Judah over the course of a decade.

---

26 1 Kings 14:14-16.
27 The story of the northern kingdom's exile is found in 2 Kings 17.
28 2 Kings 19:34.
29 Notable examples include the reforms of kings such as Hezekiah (2 Kings 18:1-20:21) and Josiah (2 Kings 22:1-23:30).
30 The repentance of Nineveh did not last. The book of **Nahum** is the "book" that Jonah wishes he had written, which condemns Nineveh and predicts Assyria's downfall.

A Babylonian warrior-king named Nebuchadnezzar invades Jerusalem and installs a puppet-king whom he can control. But after a handful of years—when the puppet king gets a little rebellious—he returns to reconquer Jerusalem.[31] And the second time that the Babylonians come to Jerusalem is far worse than anyone could have imagined.

Nebuchadnezzar lays siege to Jerusalem for two-and-a-half years, weakening its resolve and starving its population. Eventually he and his armies burst into the city and *set fire to the temple of the LORD, the royal palace and all the houses of Jerusalem. Every important building he burned down.*[32]

It's the year 586BC, and Solomon's grand city still shines brightly on its hill. This time in flames. The invading army tears down the city's walls brick by brick. The people are being deported and taken into exile to Babylon.

Looking over their shoulders as they march eastward, the people of Judah can see the temple of Yahweh billowing with smoke. The horror of reality hits them—the temple of Yahweh has been utterly destroyed.

What on earth could this mean? How could the temple of the one, true and living God lie smoldering in ashes?

The pervading attitude of the people assumed that they would live in Jerusalem forever. After all, they thought, no harm could come to Jerusalem; nothing could happen to the temple of the true and living God.[33]

But they were wrong.

---

[31] 1 Kings 23:36-25:21.
[32] 2 Kings 25:9.
[33] Jer 7:3-11.

Yahweh had warned them through the prophet Jeremiah:

"Flee for safety, people of Benjamin! Flee from Jerusalem!...For disaster looms out of the north, even terrible destruction. I will destroy Daughter Zion, so beautiful and delicate."[34]

Yahweh is smack in the middle of shattering Israel's worldview. This decimation of Jerusalem and Yahweh's temple will haunt them for centuries.

We can hear their immediate convulsions of pain in the tear-soaked poems of **Lamentations**.[35] It mourns the siege and fall of Jerusalem. But we also catch glimpses of their angst, longing and confusion in other places, as in some of the psalms:

By the rivers of Babylon we sat and wept,
when we remembered Zion.
There on the poplars we hung our harps,
for there our captors asked us for songs,
our tormentors demanded songs of joy;
they said, "Sing us one of the songs of Zion!"
How can we sing the songs of the LORD
while in a foreign land?[36]

As the people of Judah march into Babylon—into exile—they mourn, wail and groan. Life wasn't supposed to be like this. But they had rebelled against the stipulations of Sinai for centuries. Now they must endure the curse of Deuteronomy 28.

---

34 Jer 6:1-2.
35 The five chapters of the "book" of Lamentations are actually five different poems reflecting on the fall of Jerusalem. The center of the book (3:21-33) serves as its climatic, hope-filled prayer in the midst of judgment.
36 Psalm 137:1-4.

The survivors of Judah have been banished east of Jerusalem just as humanity was banished east of Eden. And the dark irony is that Abraham's descendants are headed right back to Abraham's original homeland.

They're on their way back to Ur.
They're headed to Babylon.

But the book of Kings does not end with mourning—there is still a silver lining, even to this thunderhead. Because its last four verses tell us that the king of Judah is still alive.

And he's not in critical condition.

No, the king of Judah is being treated well and eating at the king of Babylon's table.[37]

Yahweh is full of mercy.
There is still a descendant of David on the throne.

Yahweh may fulfill his promises yet.

---

[37] 2 Kings 25:27-30.

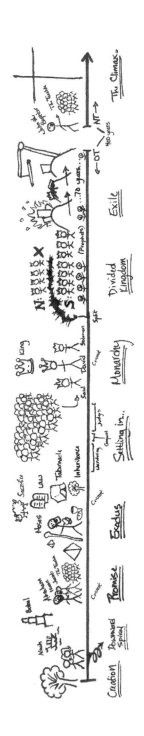

Creation

Downward Spiral

Noah
Babel

Promise
Covenant

Abraham/Sarah
The Twelve

Exodus
Covenant

Moses
Sacrifice
Law
Tabernacle
Inheritance

Settling in...
Covenant

Wandering
Conquest
Judges

Monarchy
Covenant

Saul
David
Solomon
King

Divided Kingdom

Split

N:
S:
(Prophets)

Exile

...70 years...

←OT
NT→
460 years

John the Baptist
The Twelve

The Climax

09 curse of exile

The "golden age" of Israel has crumbled. The survivors of Judah are marching toward Babylon—devastated and exiled from the land of promise. The Babylonians have conquered the South, just as the Assyrians conquered the North. But the Israelites shouldn't be surprised. The stipulations Moses announced back at Sinai were crystal clear— they would remain in the land as long as they were actually being Yahweh's holy nation. But now they rejected their task, so they have been ejected.

Now the land has vomited them out.[1]
They have been cursed with exile.

But what now of the promise to David of a never-ending dynasty?
And what of the promise to Abraham of a world-wide blessing?

Has Yahweh abandoned his people?
Has the Creator given up? Is Eden gone forever?

As the surviving Israelites begin to arrive in Babylon, they turn to prophets to help them wrestle through these tough questions.
One these prophets is named **Habakkuk**, and one particular idea haunted him: the fact that Yahweh is using the Babylonians to judge

---

1 Lev 18:24-28.

Judah.[2] But how can Yahweh bring judgment on his people by using a wicked people?

How can this be justice on any level?[3]

And Habakkuk, much like us, does not get exhaustive answers to the questions that trouble him. Rather Yahweh turns his attention to how his people ought be living by declaring *"the righteous person will live by his faithfulness."*[4]

God's people must continue to live in obedient trust to him, especially during this terrible judgment by the Babylonians. And eventually Habakkuk does just that, choosing to praise Yahweh even in the darkness of exile.[5]

But walking in obedient trust will look different here in Babylon.

When the Israelites were elected at Sinai they were given the law, the tabernacle, the sacrifices—and obedience meant that they could dwell in the land of promise. These gifts were intended to equip them to bless the nations.

But these gifts had been abused in their hands.

The temple became *"a den of robbers"* that they considered their personal fortress against both harm and against outsiders.[6] The sacrifices in the temple became a circus of religious lies performed by

---

[2] 2 Kings 24:3, Hab 1:5-11.

[3] Hab 1:13.

[4] Hab 2:4b As noted in many Bibles, "faithfulness" can also be translated "faith." Faith *in* something would naturally result in faithfulness *to* it, and the word used encompasses both. We'll be using the phrase "obedient trust" frequently, trying to get at both.

[5] Hab 3:17-19.

[6] Jer 7:9-11 as an example.

selfish, unjust people.[7] The land intended to be an oasis of light had actually become a cesspool of darkness.[8]

Now almost all of these gifts have been torn away from them. The temple, the sacrifices, and the land are gone.

The only thing left is Yahweh's law.

So obedient trust in the midst of exile means following Yahweh's instruction and trusting that Yahweh will one day fulfill his promises in surprising ways. They have to trust that one day blessing will return to Israel—and to the world.

As the exiles begin settling down in Babylon, a buzz begins to grow. Some silver-tongued, self-appointed "prophets" start to declare that Yahweh will not keep the Israelites in exile very long.

This vicious Babylonian vacation will end sooner rather than later.

Jeremiah, among the few left in Jerusalem, sends a letter to those who are in Babylon and says the opposite. They must settle down in Babylon; they must not listen to these lies.[9] Yahweh does know the plans he has for the Israelites—plans to prosper them and not to harm them; he does plan a bright hope and a future for them as a people.[10] The Israelites will indeed return to the land.

Seventy years from now.[11]
Exile is going to last a while.

---

7 Amos 5:21-27 as an example.
8 Hosea 4:1-3 as an example.
9 Jer 29:1-9.
10 Jer 29:11. Definitely a "T-shirt verse" worth reading and understanding in context.
11 Jer 29:10.

Most of the Israelites looking for national restoration within their lifetime are going to be devastated. Yahweh is patient and working on his own timetable.

Hope and a future.

Yes. Absolutely.
Without doubt.

He will restore them and fulfill their national mission.
He will indeed bless and renew all creation through them.

And they—as individuals—are invited into that cosmic renewal.

But most of them are going to die on foreign soil.

After the rescue from Egypt, a disobedient generation of Israelites had to spend the rest of their lives wandering the wilderness. And now after exile from Jerusalem, a disobedient generation of Israelites must spend the rest of their lives living in Babylon.

But as a nation, they have every reason to hope.
Yahweh will not abandon Israel to destruction and disobedience.

And as individuals, they have every reason to hope.
Yahweh will not abandoned creation to decay and death.

As a nation, they are experiencing the judgment that the prophets had warned about as early as Moses! Voices throughout their long history had warned that Israel would eventually go wildly off its tracks in rebellion and fall under a curse.[12]

---

12 Deut 28:64-68.

Right now, the people of God don't have to be convinced that they are under a curse. As they gaze into the Babylonian sunset, they need reminding—and convincing—that Yahweh can be trusted.

That God is full of surprising mercy and restores again and again.

Even on the other side of curses.[13]
Especially on the other side of curses.

And so Yahweh uses the prophets again as megaphones—this time as megaphones of hope. Through the words of prophets like Isaiah, Jeremiah and Ezekiel, God makes almost embarrassingly excessive promises about what he is going to do in the future.

Isaiah speaks comfort to the nation: *A voice of one calling:"In the wilderness prepare the way for the LORD; make straight in the desert a highway for our God..."*[14] He paints the picture of a highway being cleared in the desert which Yahweh will use to lead the people out of this cursed exile and back into intimate blessing with him. In a riveting series of chapters, Isaiah declares that the exiles and Yahweh will return to Jerusalem—healing all the brokenness, righting the wrongs, bringing justice, blessing the nations and eventually climaxing in a new heavens and a new earth.[15] And all of this flows from the obedience of Yahweh's mysterious "servant" who gives himself up for others.[16]

According to Isaiah, not only is Yahweh not done with Israel, he's also working through the suffering of exile of the nation and his servant for the renewal of all creation.

---

13 The hope of restoration after curse is emphasized in Deut 30:1-6.
14 Isa 40:3.
15 Read Isa 40-66 (especially 52-55) with this in mind and get swept up in it. It's absolutely riveting.
16 Isa 52:13-53:12.

Jeremiah also speaks hope to the people. He promises that Yahweh will make a "new covenant" with his people. The people of Israel, after all, broke the stipulations of the two-sided covenant made at Sinai.[17] But this "new covenant" will be different from the deal at Sinai. Yahweh will actually embed his instruction *within* his people. He will forgive their sins —both national and personal—to ensure that they can obey and choose life.[18]

According to Jeremiah, Yahweh will restore his people through a new covenant that will be as one-sided, sure-thing and fool-proof as the promises he made to Abraham and David.

Ezekiel becomes a prophet as the exile is beginning, and he speaks with some of the most colorful (and downright bizarre) imagery in all the Bible. His early words, before the siege and fall of Jerusalem, sharply criticize the people of Judah. But after the temple falls, he won't shut up about Yahweh's plan to renew them.[19] In an iconic passage, he envisions the nation as utterly and hopelessly dead—a valley of dusty bones. And yet Yahweh breathes his Spirit into these dead bones, making them live once again.[20]

According to Ezekiel, the Creator who breathed into dirt when he first created humanity will also breathe into the bones of his people to recreate and "resurrect" his people.

---

[17] Remember that the covenants with Abraham and David were one-sided. With each of them, Yahweh was making unconditional promises, so there was nothing to break there.

[18] Jer 31:31-34.

[19] The turning point in Ezekiel is 33:21, when the temple falls. The language of sharp judgment that dominates the beginning of the book is replaced with rich restoration at the end. As an example, contrast chapter 16 with chapter 36.

[20] Ezk 37:1-14.

The prophets are united in their message—Yahweh is not finished with creation and therefore he is not finished with Israel. Yahweh will do something absolutely amazing in the future.

Yahweh is good. And he is full of surprises.

But for now, the Israelites are exiled in Babylon.
Seventy years in exile.

Which brings us back to the question:
how does one live in exile?

What does obedient trust to Yahweh look like?

Jeremiah's letter recommends that the Israelites settle down, live quietly and pray that Yahweh will bless this foreign city, nation and people. As crazy as it sounds, they are to pray to Yahweh for the prosperity of Babylon.[21]

Yet other voices in Scripture challenge the Israelites into another necessary posture during exile:

Resistance.

Set during this time period of exile, the book of **Daniel** warns Israel not to compromise with its foreign captors. The book begins relatively small, with Daniel and his friends refusing to eat unclean food.[22] But the stories escalate, the stakes grow and situations become increasingly dangerous.

---

21 Jer 29:5-7.
22 Dan 1:1-20. The dietary laws of Israel are one of the absolute distinguishing marks of being a Jew. The other two are circumcision and keeping the Sabbath.

Daniel's friends reject idolatry, even in the face of a fiery death.[23]
Daniel himself refuses to pray to the Persian king as a god and finds
himself thrown into a den of lions.[24]

But instead of enduring horrible deaths, Daniel and his friends are all
rescued by Yahweh. Throughout the book of Daniel, foreign powers are
shown to be fools and Yahweh to be the true King—not only over Israel
but also over all the nations.[25]

"Resist and do not compromise with these oppressors!"
"These foreign rulers do not deserve our allegiance!"
"There is only one King who deserves our loyalty!"

Daniel's stories of resistance are also paired with visions of Yahweh's
kingdom finally being reestablished on earth. These revelations and
dreams are as strange and puzzling as some of our own dreams.

One dream involves a giant statue made of many types of materials
finally being replaced by a grand mountain.[26]

Another involves a succession of beastly, sub-human kingdoms finally
being replaced by the kingdom of "*one like a son of man.*"[27] The world is
full of vicious rulers and kingdoms that are less-than-human, that are like
animals and beasts. But they will one day be replaced by God's kingdom
—a reign that will reveal what true humanity is all about.

Still another vision involves an angel named Gabriel announcing to
Daniel that this kingdom is coming soon.[28]

---

23 Dan 3:1-27.
24 Dan 6.
25 Dan 2:47, 3:28-29, 4:34-37.
26 Dan 2.
27 Dan 7. The mysterious "one like a son of man" who is ascending toward God is found in 7:13.
28 Dan 9:20-24.

"Hold on! Remain faithful!"

"Walk in obedient trust!"

"The rule and reign of Yahweh is coming!"

And so the Israelites live in the tension of exile, praying for the blessing of Babylon while also resisting its beastly charms.

And still another struggle in the midst of exile is that of suffering. Here the Israelites may have taken solace in the story of **Job**. Like Job, Israel suffers because they had been singled out, chosen, elected for the purpose of blessing the world. Job was singled out because he was upright—his suffering no fault of his own.[29] While this is certainly different than the well-deserved exile of Israelites, it probes Israel with good questions:

Should they curse God and die?

Or should they accept both good and trouble from God?[30]

The book of Job offers no easy answers, and Israel's present position in exile allows for none. But Job's story does insist that relentless trust in the goodness and justice of God is well-placed, especially when suffering dominates the story. And it whispers that justice, renewal and resurrection come for those who continue to humbly trust Yahweh.[31]

And so they wait.

For years.

In the tension of praying for Babylon and resisting Babylon.

In the struggle of suffering.

29 Job 1:8, 22; 2:3.
30 Job 2:9-10.
31 Job 42:7-17 is certainly a "resurrection" of sorts for Job.

And after decades of praying, resisting and suffering, finally light begins to emerge—the dawn begins to break.

Yahweh finally makes a move.

Time has been marching on, and the Babylonian empire has now fallen to the advancing Persian empire. Yahweh raises up a Persian king by the name of Cyrus to send the Israelites back to their land, just as Isaiah had predicted.[32]

Persia is a beastly empire, but Yahweh has it on a leash.

Yahweh raises up a pagan king for the purpose of conquering Babylon and sending his people back to Jerusalem. And in the year 538BC, Cyrus issues a decree to the exiles:

Return to Jerusalem!
They are finally free to go home!

To the land of their parents, and grandparents and ancestors!
To the land promised to Abraham, Isaac and Jacob!

This decree by Cyrus is actually the way that the book of **Chronicles** ends.[33] Jeremiah had predicted that the Israelites would be in Babylon for 70 years, and Yahweh is true to his word.

"So grab the bags and lace your sandals! We're headed back to Jerusalem! We're headed back to the land! We're headed home!"

---

[32] Isa 45:1-14.

[33] 2 Chr 36:20-23. The book of **Chronicles** (it's divided into two parts in our Bibles for the sake of reading and reference) is actually a retelling of the Israel's history from Genesis to Kings from the perspective of *after* the return to Jerusalem.

Israel must feel like Yahweh is finally restoring the kingdom of Israel and establishing the kingdom of God. That they are marching that highway through the desert. That Yahweh is establishing that new covenant right now. That their dry bones are finally coming alive again. That the curse of exile is finally coming to an end.

But Yahweh is patient and working on his own timetable.

And he is full of surprises.

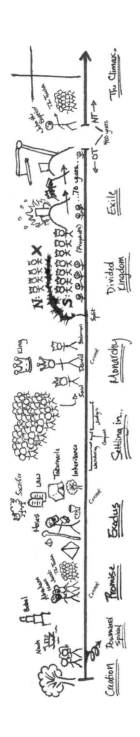

Creation · Downward Spiral · Promise · Exodus · Settling in... · Monarchy · Divided Kingdom · Exile · The Climax

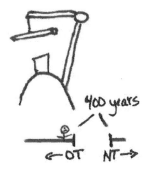

400 years

OT → ← NT →

10 anticipation

The Israelites are finally on their way back home; they are finally headed back to Jerusalem. With seventy years of exile in Babylon finally behind them, they are certain that brighter days are ahead. Their ancestors' stubborn scorn for the ancient stipulations of Sinai had left them under a curse. But now that curse seems to be ending. Perhaps this will finally be the generation in which Yahweh fulfills his expanding list of promises made to Abraham, David and through the prophets.

World-wide blessing.
A never-ending dynasty.

Renewed creation.
New covenant.

A resurrected nation.

Yahweh definitely is at work. After all, Persia conquered Babylon, and Cyrus issued the decree that they should return to Jerusalem. They're headed home.

So is the curse over? Are promises being fulfilled?
Is the long exile ending? Is blessing coming?

All they can do is return to Jerusalem and trust.

All they can is rebuild and resettle. And pray.

This period of Israel's history is recorded in the books of **Ezra** and **Nehemiah**.[1] That decree from Cyrus which ended the book of Chronicles is actually how the book of Ezra starts:

By official royal decree of the king of Persia, the Israelites are to return to their land and rebuild the temple in Jerusalem.[2] He even loads their bags with various treasures that old Nebuchadnezzar had plundered from Solomon's temple.[3] They're headed back, loaded down with sacks of gold.

Land, check.

A man by the name of Zerubbabel is leading these enthusiastic Israelites through the desert back to their land.[4] And the air is electric with excitement because Zerubbabel is from the line of David.[5] So they're returning with a "son of David" at the helm.

Potential king, check.

When they arrive, they find only a shell of the once-gleaming city of Solomon. Jerusalem lies largely in ruins. So first things first, Zerubbabel joins with the high priest to rebuild Yahweh's altar so the people can resume sacrificing to Yahweh.[6]

---

[1] Ezra and Nehemiah were likely originally one work ("Ezra-Nehemiah"). They tell one full account and should be read together.
[2] Ezra 1:1-4.
[3] Ezra 1:7. See also 2 Kings 24:13.
[4] e.g. Ezra 2:2, 4:2.
[5] 1 Ch 3:19, Hag 2:20-23.
[6] Ezra 3:1-6.

Sacrifices, check.

Then they begin rebuilding the temple.[7] During the exile, Ezekiel had envisioned the glorious presence of Yahweh leaving his temple in Jerusalem to travel with his people into Babylon while they endured exile.[8] Rebuilding the temple would be a sign to the world that Yahweh had not abandoned them. Perhaps the glorious presence of Yahweh will return to the temple.

But after the foundation of the temple is laid, there's a heart-wrenching mixed reaction—celebration and weeping. An excited younger generation can barely contain their enthusiasm. They're finally rebuilding the temple they have heard and dreamt about their entire lives. But the very oldest among them break down in tears. They still remember the grandeur of Solomon's grand temple.[9]

And this is nothing like that.

But under the direction of Zerubbabel and the high priest—and with a few strong kicks in the pants from prophets such as **Haggai** and **Zechariah**—the temple is finally completed.[10]

Temple, check.

Now enter Ezra. He's a priest who intensely studied the law of Moses during the waning years of exile. He travels from Babylon to Jerusalem with a single purpose—to instruct the Israelites what it means to truly be

---

7 Ezra 3:7-13.

8 Ezk 9:3, 10:4, 10:18, 11:23. The hope was that Yahweh's glory would one day return to a glorious and rebuilt temple in the land (e.g. Ezk 43:4).

9 Ezra 3:11-13.

10 Ezra 5:1-2 and 6:13-15. Construction on the temple is temporarily stopped in 4:24 because of complaints from the Israelites' northern neighbors—those with whom Assyria had repopulated the northern kingdom (4:1-23). After some politicking and a regime change in Persia, the temple-building is recommenced in Jerusalem—this time with Persian tax-dollars funding it (6:8)!

Israel.[11] A new generation is relearning what it means to live as Yahweh's chosen people on behalf of the world.[12]

Law, check.

If you're keeping score at home, the Israelites are checking off all the right boxes:

Land. Davidic king. Sacrifices. Temple. Law.

Checks all around.

They really want to see Yahweh fulfill his promises.
Preferably this generation, because they're sick of waiting.

The people recognize that Yahweh brought them back to the land, and they're going to try to avoid any potential pitfall this time.

Nehemiah stands out as another significant figure in this period. He is an Israelite who serves as cupbearer to the Persian king. From his high position, he requests permission to return to Jerusalem; he desperately wants to rebuild its walls.[13] This makes perfect sense because walls were one of the most important parts of any ancient city—your primary means of defense. Nehemiah knows that without walls, Jerusalem doesn't stand a chance of staying rebuilt for long.

The king of Persia grants Nehemiah's request to go and spearhead this effort. Rebuilding of the walls faces some fierce opposition—just like the

---

11 Ezra 7:6-10. His journey to Jerusalem is described in Ezra 8:15-36.
12 See Ezra 9-10 and Nehemiah 8 for examples.
13 Neh 1:1-2:10.

rebuilding of the temple did—but Nehemiah persists and eventually succeeds in fortifying Jerusalem against attack.[14]

Together, these two men rebuild different parts of Israel:

Nehemiah rebuilds the physical infrastructure of Jerusalem.
Ezra rebuilds the spiritual infrastructure of Jerusalem.

But both Nehemiah and Ezra recognize that this "return" may not be exactly what Israel had been hoping for. After all, Yahweh's promises were colossal and world-changing. Their present situation—possessing the land but under Persian control—seems like just a different sort of slavery. Another kind of captivity. It seems like they've returned from Babylon but not from exile.

They've returned to the land,
they're rebuilding the temple,
they're offering plenty of sacrifices
and they're strenuously following Yahweh's instruction.

But they're still in exile.[15]

Because the ancient promises made to Abraham and David don't seem to be reality yet. The sweeping promises made through Isaiah, Jeremiah, Ezekiel and the rest of the prophets will surely look different than this when they are fulfilled. Questions grow as the weeks and months turn into years and decades:

"Could this really be the new covenant? We kinda doubt it. After all, where is the kingdom and the king? Where is new creation? We don't

---

14 Neh 6:15. Opposition arrises in both chapter 4 and chapter 6.
15 Ezra 9:8-9, Neh 9:36-37.

feel blessed. And we certainly don't feel like we've experienced any kind of resurrection."

With these nagging questions, it's difficult to trust.

But trust they must:

That Yahweh is righteous (that is, he will act rightly).[16]
That Yahweh is faithful. That Yahweh is in control.

The entire book of **Esther** quietly testifies to the faithfulness and power of Yahweh—that he can and should be trusted. Set during the reign of the Persian empire, this short story is loaded with dramatic irony and intrigue. It tells how Esther winds up becoming queen of the Persian Empire. And from this position, she saves her people—the Jews[17]—from a conspiracy bent on annihilating them. All of this can be recognized as the powerful, protective and providential hand of Yahweh.[18]

Yahweh is righteous. Yahweh is faithful. Yahweh is in control.
And Yahweh will fulfill his grand promises when the time is right. After all, he has been faithful from Egypt to Esther. Now they must wait patiently on him. Even though it still feels like slavery, they must live in obedient trust, just as Habakkuk said.[19]

As this period of waiting and trusting gets longer and longer, however, it becomes evident that the people's hearts may not have changed much.

---

[16] See Daniel's prayer in Dan 9:4-19 for a great example of trusting in the righteousness of God (9:7). Yahweh's character is one that does right. This meant bringing judgment on them when that was needed (9:14) but it's also their ground for asking for mercy (9:16).

[17] It is during the Persian empire that the Israelites become known by the name of the region they live in —Judah. This is why they are not called "Jews" until Ezra, Nehemiah, Esther, etc.

[18] The theme of providence becomes even more powerful when we recognize that neither the word "God" nor the name "Yahweh" appear in the story! He is absolutely assumed.

[19] Hab 2:4.

This generation returning to the land is struggling with the same problems as generations past.

An example is marrying foreigners and allowing them to sway their allegiance to Yahweh. Sound familiar? That was precisely one of Solomon's downfalls—his foreign wives swayed his heart. Ezra and Nehemiah try to address this problem head-on.[20] But they also know that this is merely a symptom of the people still-corrupt hearts. The new covenant still hasn't come yet.

Malachi, the last prophet chronologically in the Old Testament, recognizes this symptom too. In his day, the issue has become such a problem that Israelite men are divorcing their Jewish wives to marry foreign women.[21] *"The man who hates and divorces his wife," says the* LORD, *the God of Israel, "does violence to the one he should protect."*[22]

And this isn't the only symptom that Malachi sees. He also condemns Israel's sloppy sacrifices, corrupt priests, continued social injustice and robbing the temple of what it was due.[23] The Jewish people have returned from exile, but they're showing the same symptoms they always have.

A growing majority in Israel is becoming disillusioned:

What good is there in serving Yahweh?[24]
Doubts abound whether Yahweh has returned to the temple.[25]

---

20 Ezra 9:1-10:17; Neh 13:23-27.
21 Mal 2:10-15.
22 Mal 2:16. This verse can also be translated, *"I hate divorce," says the* LORD, *the God of Israel,* *"because the man who divorces his wife covers his garment with violence."* In either case, what is happening in v10-15 is seen as absolutely unacceptable.
23 Sloppy sacrifices = Mal 1:6-14; corrupt priests = Mal 2:1-9; continued injustice = Mal 2:17 & 3:5; robbing temple = Mal 3:8-12.
24 Mal 3:14.
25 Mal 3:6-7. In Ezk 8-11, Ezekiel has a vision of Yahweh's glory leaving the temple as the Babylonians loomed large on the horizon.

Surely it should look different than this, and Malachi insists that it will. He declares that Yahweh will indeed return to his temple.[26] In fact, a messenger like wild-eyed Elijah will prepare the way for him.[27]

Rest assured Yahweh will come, fulfilling all his promises.

And with these warnings and promises from Malachi the Old Testament goes silent.[28] Four hundred years of silence from Yahweh.

* * *

That's not to say that we've got 400 years of missing history. We have plenty of writings from these centuries. Many call them "inter-testamental writings" because they are from between the Old and New Testaments. They allow us to understand how the story of the Jewish people continues to take shape.

After a century of Persian rule, Israel's story collides with an incredibly ambitious young man named Alexander of Macedon.[29] He is the son of King Philip of Macedon and studies under some of the most brilliant minds of the day (one of his tutors is a fellow named Aristotle). He inherits his assassinated father's throne when he is only twenty. Around a decade later, he has conquered the known world.[30] That includes conquering the Persian empire along with the Jewish subjects it ruled. This is enough to secure him celebrity status and name recognition down to this day. He is remembered as Alexander the Great.

---

26 Mal 3:1. This squares with Zechariah's vision in Zech 9:9-17 of Yahweh coming as a shepherd to save his flock of people. In that vision, he's a victorious king riding a lowly donkey.

27 Mal 3:1a, 4:5.

28 This is, of course, from a Protestant perspective. The Catholic and Orthodox Churches affirm a handful of intertestamental writings (called the deuterocanonical books) as authoritative and a part of their Old Testaments.

29 Macedon was just north of modern-day Greece.

30 1 Maccabees 1:1-4. I am indebted to a variety of scholars here, not least of which is F.F. Bruce, *Israel and the Nations*, 116-118 and N.T. Wright, *The New Testament and the People of God*, 157-159.

It is important for our purposes to recognize that as Alexander conquers various territories he is spreading Greek culture. The Western world is becoming "Hellenized."[31] This means that a common culture, currency and language spreads across the wide expanse of the known world.[32] The world becomes Greek-flavored.

The book of **Daniel** speaks of this period with cryptic images, describing a *"mighty king"* from the *"kingdom of Greece."*[33] He tells how this king will have no heir and how his kingdom would be divided up after his death.[34] Sure enough, after Alexander's death his kingdom winds up being divided among those closest to him.[35]

Tracing the generals, empires, battles and backstabbing that follow the division of Alexander's kingdom is (thankfully) beyond the scope of this book. We're interested in the redemptive story that God has worked in and through Abraham's family. So let's return to them:

During this time of "hellenization," some of the Jewish people align themselves culturally with the nations (also called "gentiles") surrounding them. If you can't beat them, join them. They secure a Greek education, hide their circumcision through surgery and essentially abandon all that distinguishes them as Jewish.[36]

But not everyone bows to the pressure of prevailing culture in the centuries following Alexander.[37] That's not the only response on the

---

31 The Greeks did not call themselves Greek ("graecos") but rather called themselves "Hellenes." The name that the Romans will later give them (Greeks or "graecos") will be the one that sticks.
32 Which included the eastern part of the Mediterranean coast from Greece to northern Africa, the Middle East, some of modern-day Turkey, and outposts as far as India.
33 Dan 11:2-3.
34 Dan 11:4.
35 1 Maccabees 1:5-9, F.F. Bruce, *Israel and the Nations* (Downers Grove, IL: IVP Press,1997), 119-120.
36 1 Maccabees 1:11-15.
37 The kingdoms of the Ptolemies and the Seleucids are the most relevant because they overlap Jewish territory. These are the kingdoms that put the most pressure on the Jews to conform—especially the Seleucids.

table. Many cling to the promises of Yahweh for hope. Daniel's visions of Yahweh's coming kingdom become a popular rallying point. As they watch kingdoms come and go, they remember his visions of beastly, inhumane kingdoms rising and falling—and then finally being replaced with a the kingdom of *one like the son of man*.[38]

A human kingdom at last.
A humane kingdom at last.

The good Creator ruling through his people once again.

Many faithfully trust that the promises of Yahweh will be fulfilled, and those who have remained faithful—especially in the midst of suffering—will participate in the new life of the kingdom of God.

This belief naturally led to incredible anticipation about *how* precisely Yahweh was going to establish this kingdom. But no consensus could be found about how this would happen.

Despite modern misconceptions, there was never a checklist of characteristics or responsibilities for the "Messiah" (or "Anointed One" or "Christ") who would liberate Israel from foreign rule.[39] In fact, at this point all kinds of Jews are aiming to redeem Israel. Many aspire to be Yahweh's tool for bringing about the fulfillment of his promises.[40]

Many try.

---

38 Daniel 7:1-28.
39 I am indebted here to the scholarship of N.T. Wright, *The New Testament and the People of God* (Minneapolis: Fortress Press, 1992), 281-338.
40 Much of their efforts were focused on bringing about the promise to David (kingdom) rather than the promise to Abraham (blessing the world).

One family called the Maccabees
actually manages to succeed for a century.[41]

But nothing lasts long.

Hardly an everlasting kingdom.

After that brief century of relative independence, Israel is once again
conquered by another foreign superpower. This time it's a new empire
originating from the Apennine Peninsula (modern day Italy). This empire
sweeps in from the West through the fractured remnants of Alexander's
empire and finds a lot that's useful. Being practical people, they keep
much of the Greek language and culture in place—after all, why mess
with a good thing? Then they extend their legal system into these new
territories and build incredible miles of stone roads to ease the
transportation of their massive army. Within their ever-increasing
borders, they succeed in promoting transportation, trade, communication
and peace.

The known world becomes united under their king—Caesar.

The rule of the Roman Empire has arrived.

And now, in light of all Rome's glitz and grandeur, the promises of the
prophets are starting to look rather ragged and pathetic. Sure, Israel
returned from physical captivity but they're still in exile, now under the
control of the Romans.

They still long for the promises of the prophets to be fulfilled:

---

[41] The Maccabean revolt in 166 BC succeeded in winning Jewish independence from the Seleucid
Empire. The books of 1 & 2 Maccabees tell this story. Their successors (called the Hasmonean dynasty)
managed to keep themselves free of foreign rule until they were conquered by the Roman general
Pompey in 63 BC.

Where is this renewed creation?
The new covenant?
The resurrection of Israel?

The promises to David (and through Daniel) also look shabby:

An everlasting kingdom? How? When? Where?
The nations have been kicking Israel around for centuries.

And what were those promises to Abraham ever even about?
The nations of the world don't need to be blessed through Abraham's
family! They seem to be doing fine on their own! Israel is the one in need
of blessing!

And it is here—in the middle of these burning questions, in the midst of
this tension and under the crushing boot of Rome—that we hear the
voice of someone crying in the wilderness.

He's preparing the way for Yahweh's coming. He's crying out:
"Repent, for the kingdom of heaven has come near."[42]

Ladies and gentlemen, I'd like you to meet John the Baptizer.

He's announcing the coming of the kingdom.
He's preparing the way for the King.

---

42 Matt 3:2.

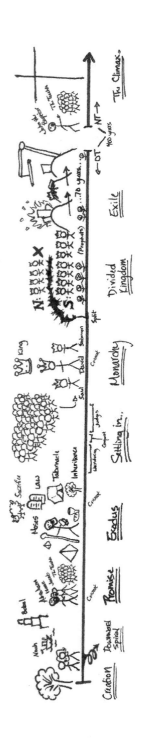

// climax part one

*** One danger (and tragedy) of this book is how much must be flattened out at the best of parts. By God's direction and wisdom, we are given four incredibly rich, remarkably different, hauntingly similar portraits of Jesus of Nazareth.[1] Listening to only one of these accounts is a bit like listening to a symphony play Mozart with only the brass or only the strings or only the percussion. We need all types of instruments playing to hear a symphony. How much more do we need all four gospels to hear the climatic crescendo of Israel's story? And at no other point does this book's inadequacy become more evident than here. What follows will be like hearing Mozart played on three banjos over a walkie talkie. Read all four gospels. For that matter, read the whole Bible. Alright, disclaimer done. ***

After centuries of waiting, the Jewish people are ready for Yahweh to act. They believe in their bones that Yahweh can. After all, he's been acting throughout their entire history:

They wouldn't even exist if Yahweh had not acted on his promise to bless Abraham. He acted again when he redeemed them from slavery to the Egyptians and gave them the promised land. Again and again he rescued them from enemies. In spite of their relentless rebellion, he promised their great king David that he would be the first in a never-ending dynasty. To be sure, Yahweh brought judgment on his rebellious people because he is the God who acts rightly. But he also promised that world-changing blessing would eventually come on the other side of the curse of exile. Yahweh has been acting throughout Israel's long history.

---

[1] For a great look at the diversity and unity of the four gospels, read *Four Gospels, One Jesus: A Portrait* by Richard Burridge (Grand Rapids: Eerdmans, 2005). Additionally, *Can We Trust the Gospels?* by Mark Roberts (Wheaton, IL: Crossway, 2007) provides an accessible defense of their historical reliability.

Now Israel is quite ready for him to act again. Because they returned from Babylon only to be kicked around for centuries by Persia, Greece and eventually Rome.

When will Yahweh act decisively?
And how will he fulfill these grand promises?

As the Hebrew Scriptures end, we realize that its story never reached its climax. But the Christian Scriptures give us one. The New Testament is not the beginning of a story. It's the climax of one, and boy is it a doozy. This is why the New Testament begins the way it does:

This is the genealogy of Jesus the Messiah, the son of David, the son of Abraham.[2]

This is not a new story. This is *that* story. That story of Abraham and David, exodus and exile, prophets and promises, rebellion and recreation. *That* story.

Yahweh is finally acting. In their different ways, all four gospels proclaim in their very openings that the promises of Yahweh are being fulfilled in Jesus.[3] All four consider Jesus' story to be the climax of Israel's story.

All four are calling Jesus "the Messiah."

Messiah (Hebrew) translates into Greek as "christos" (Christ).

Jesus is the "Anointed One."

---

[2] Matt 1:1. The Greek for "genealogy" is actually "Genesis." Matthew is picking up the thread from Gen 2:4, 5:1, 10:1 and 11:10.

[3] Matt 1:1, mentioned above, is followed by genealogies that connect the dots of Israel's history. Mk 1:1-3 ties the story in with the prophets (Isaiah & Malachi), Lk 1:1 speaks of the things fulfilled in their midst (and moves quickly into the history-laden songs of Mary and Zechariah). Jn 1:1 is the beginning of New Creation (Isa 65:17-25).

This is the story of the long-awaited King.

The king of Israel had always functioned as a representative of the people as a whole, but when Jesus shows up he does it in an unprecidented way. The entire life of Jesus embodies and retells the "life" of Israel. Here is a man taking his people's long history—and their task— entirely on his shoulders. Flashes, shadows and echoes of Israel's story resonate throughout his entire life.

Jesus is Israel as Israel was meant to be.

Before we return to John the Baptizer crying in the wilderness, three of the gospel writers give accounts of Jesus' origin.

The traditional "Christmas story" actually comes from combining Jesus' birth stories from both Matthew and Luke.[4] Each of these stories wants their readers to understand that Jesus is both from the line of David and from the Spirit of Yahweh.[5] With his signature flourish, John chooses to invoke the creation overture of Genesis to emphasize that Jesus is someone entirely unexpected and divine entering into our world.[6] The gospel of Mark alone jumps straight into the action by opening with the Baptizer.

Here all four evangelists speak together: a wild-eyed prophet cries out in the wilderness of Judaea. This Baptizer is calling Israel to turn back to obedient trust of Yahweh and is declaring someone far greater than him is coming.[7] This reminds us immediately of the final prophet, Malachi,

---

4 Matt 1:18-2:23, Luke 2:1-20.
5 David = Matt 1:1:1-17, Lk 1:27. (Mark will reference his relation to David later in his Gospel [Mk 10:47-48].) Spirit of Yahweh = Matt 1:20, Lk 1:35.
6 John 1:1-5 (compare with Gen 1:1-5).
7 Matt 3:1-12, Mk 1:1-8, Lk 3:1-20, Jn 1:6-8, 15, 19-31.

predicting that a messenger like Elijah would be announce the coming of Yahweh himself.[8]

When the curtain rises, however, Jesus takes the stage.
Which begs a question, who do the gospel-writers think Jesus is?

A good question to keep in mind.

The answer is part of why it's called the good news.

Jesus approaches this wild prophet to be baptized, and suddenly the scene becomes a royal coronation. The skies tear open and the Spirit of Yahweh descends on Jesus. We hear a voice from heaven speak loaded words over Jesus:[9]

"You are my Son, whom I love; with you I am well pleased."[10]

The words are actually a combination of both a psalm and a prophecy.[11] First, the snippet from Psalm 2 which reads: *I will proclaim the LORD's decree: He said to me, "You are my son; today I have become your father."*[12]

When a person is installed as President of the United States, there is a ceremony that takes place involving words from the Constitution. In a similar way, Israel used Psalm 2 in a ceremony celebrating a new king. Like David and his descendants after him, Jesus has taken on the royal title of "Son of God."

---

8 Mal 3:1a, 4:5.
9 Matt 3:16-17, Mk 1:9-11, Lk 3:21-22, Jn 1:32-34.
10 Mk 1:11b and Lk 3:22b (see also Matt 3:17).
11 D.A. Carson, *Matthew*, Expositor's Bible Commentary, 109-110.
12 Psalm 2:7.

To be the "Son of God" means to be the king.[13]

Second, the bit of prophecy, coming from Isaiah: *"Here is my servant, whom I uphold, my chosen one in whom I delight; I will put my Spirit on him, and he will bring justice to the nations."*[14] Only the first part (*"in whom I delight"*) is actually spoken by the heavenly voice. The rest actually gets acted out with the Spirit descending on—being put on— Jesus.

The gospels are quietly and cleverly identifying Jesus the Messiah as Isaiah's mysterious Servant who brings justice to the nations.

Jesus the King.
Jesus the Servant.

The two are inseparable.

After his baptism, the Spirit leads Jesus into the wilderness to be confronted with grueling temptation.[15] Sound familiar? Israel wandered in the wilderness for 40 years, and now Jesus endures 40 days in the wilderness—he's retracing Israel's steps.

More than that, Jesus confronts the tempter himself. He will not fall into the same rebellious patterns as Israel, and he confronts lies with the truth of Israel's law.[16] He will not be swayed by the allure of power or authority that comes through shortcuts or compromise. The scene practically screams:

---

13 For examples see 2 Sam 7:14, Psalm 2, and Psalm 89:19-37. This title of the king being the adopted son of God develops because he is the head of the Israel who itself is called God's Son (Ex 4:22, Hos 11:1). As Christians, we affirm "Son of God" to also be a way of distinguishing the Son within the Trinity. Jesus is the "Son of God," but he is also "God the Son." More technically, he's the "only-begotten" Son of God. This distinction, however, comes *after* and *because of* Jesus, not before.
14 Isa 42:1 (which ultimately leads to a crescendo of Isa 52:13-53:12).
15 Matt 4:1-11, Mk 1:12-13, Lk 4:1-13.
16 Jesus' responses in the temptation come from Deuteronomy 6:13, 6:16 and 8:3.

Jesus succeeds above and beyond where Israel failed.

He will be faithful
in every way
that Israel was not.

This servant-king will not break obedient trust in Yahweh.

After emerging from the wilderness, Jesus goes public. He begins proclaiming the good news ("gospel") to everyone in Israel:

"The time has come," he said. "The kingdom of God has come near. Repent and believe the good news!"[17]

This may strike many of us as odd, if we really stop and consider it. Many Christians primarily understand "the gospel" as centering around Jesus' death and resurrection. How can Jesus himself be proclaiming something that hasn't happened yet? The answer is that the good news —according to Jesus—is the rule and reign of Yahweh. And it has finally come near!

This creates an immediate political and religious stir:
Is this rabbi—this teacher—talking about the kingdom promised to David? That kingdom!? The rule and reign of Yahweh through his anointed king? Finally arriving?

If it were true, that would be incredible news!

In his first hometown sermon, Jesus stands up and reads from Isaiah:
"The Spirit of the Lord is on me, because he has anointed me to proclaim

---

[17] Mk 1:15. See also Matthew 4:17. As a side note, the gospel of Matthew is likely written to the most Jewish Christians and carries over the Israelite hesitancy to speak the name of God. Rather than saying the kingdom of God, Matthew almost always says "kingdom of heaven."

good news to the poor. He has sent me to proclaim freedom for the prisoners and recovery of sight for the blind, to set the oppressed free, to proclaim the year of the Lord's favor."[18]

These words from Isaiah declare how the curse of exile will finally end, and Yahweh will finally reign over the world through his anointed king. And when that happens, this will be good news for anyone desperate and humble enough to long for his reign. After he reads these words, Jesus proclaims that these words have now been fulfilled.[19]

What an announcement! This is indeed good news!
It's what the Jewish people have been waiting on for centuries!

But Jesus is not simply content to *announce* the kingdom of God. He is actually *establishing* the kingdom around him. The reign of Yahweh radiates out from Jesus—fulfilling the words of Isaiah in a very literal sense. The blind, the poor, the oppressed—they all meet Jesus and walk away rejoicing. Jesus walks around healing the broken, banishing evil, raising the dead.

He is the King and Servant who simply speaks to makes things around him as they should be. Wherever Jesus is present, so is the rule and reign of Yahweh, the Creator.

His kingdom is good,
it's good, it's very good.

These miracles are incredible to be sure, but they're not necessarily uncharted territory. Plenty of other figures had done similar miracles.

---

18 Lk 4:18-19.
19 Lk 4:21.

Elisha multiplied food and cleansed a leper.[20] Both he and his mentor, Elijah, had even raised the dead.[21]

Miracles are incredible, yes,
but not unprecedented.

But his miraculous signs are accompanied by his teaching.

Jesus forces his fellow Jews to reexamine and sometimes radically rethink their assumptions about Yahweh's kingdom. Sometimes he reaffirms Israel's task to be a holy nation in rather stringent and straightforward ways.[22] But very often he teaches them in another way— subversive stories.

Jesus does not tell these stories (called parables) as cute illustrations to simply try to make things clearer. In fact, he claims to be using these stories to confuse certain people.[23] Some within Israel have hardened themselves and arrogantly assume they have Yahweh and his kingdom figured out. The parables will perplex the proud. But those humble, desperate and receptive enough to be taught—those people will understand.

You see, different factions had developed within the nation—all with stubbornly different opinions about how Yahweh's kingdom would come about. We could summarize three of them quickly:

---

[20] 2 Kings 4:42-44 & 5:1-14.

[21] 2 Kings 4:8-37 and 1 Kings 17:7-24.

[22] The most obvious example of Jesus' teaching and reinterpretation of the law is found in the "sermon on the mount" in Matt 5-7.

[23] In Matt 13:11-17, Mk 4:10-12 and Lk 8:9-10, Jesus invokes Isaiah 6 as the method behind (at least some of) his parables. Chapter 6 of Isaiah is where the prophet Isaiah is being called to warn Israel about the impending judgment of exile. Yahweh tells Isaiah that despite his warnings, they will not listen.

The Pharisees (following the example of figures like Ezra) thought that Yahweh must be waiting for the Jewish people to finally follow his instruction more fully. Then he will fulfill his promises and establish his kingdom. So try harder!

The Zealots assumed that Yahweh's kingdom would eventually come through Israel winning through military might. It had worked for a century with the Maccabees before Rome came—maybe it could work again. Yahweh will work through violent revolution. So take up arms!

Finally, the Sadducees were the official religious leaders (including the priesthood maintaining the temple) who had become wealthy, content and corrupt. In their eyes, maybe the kingdom of Rome isn't all that bad —Yahweh's kingdom might even come through it. Either way, we've got a good thing going. So don't rock the boat!

But for all their differences, they all shared one thing in common. They all agreed what a real kingdom should look like—Rome.
When Yahweh finally does away with these foreign rulers, Israel as God's chosen, elected people will be at the top. Rome had became their image of the kingdom. In their minds, the reign of the Son of Man would look similar to the way the beastly kingdoms rule. That's all they've known for centuries, so that must be all there is. Israel *ruling* the world instead of Israel *blessing* the world.

Jesus will have none of this—everyone is misguided in their methods and mistaken about what the kingdom will look like.

The Pharisees and their nit-picking observance of the law have actually missed the bigger point of the law.[24] Their merciless religion crushes life rather than giving it. Apologies, Zealots, but you've got to love your

---

24 e.g. Matt 23:23 (the whole chapter is an example though).

enemies while prayerfully seeking the kingdom.[25] The kingdom will not come through weapons and war. Finally, a big "no" to the Sadducees. The kingdom of Rome is not bringing about the kingdom of God.[26]

Jesus teaches about Yahweh's kingdom in entirely different terms than his contemporaries. And so he goes a step further—he establishes a symbolically new people of God within the old one. Out of his many disciples he chooses twelve to be his apostles, or special messengers.[27]

Twelve!? Really!? Yahweh had originally formed the nation of Israel out of Jacob's twelve sons, centering them around himself. And now Jesus—this rabbi from Nazareth, for crying out loud!—is forming a new Israel around himself.

The symbolism is absolutely loaded. Might this not be a bit too far? Creating a new Israel would be a job for Yahweh alone!

Who is this man daring to call out a new twelve?[28]
Who is this man claiming to fulfill Scripture?[29]

Who is this man teaching with authority?[30]
Who is this man who can forgive sins?[31]

---

25 Matt 5:43-48, 6:9-13, 33.
26 Matt 20:25, Mk 10:42.
27 Matt 10:1-4, Mk 3:13-19, Lk 6:12-16 (Jn 6:67 introduces the twelve as those disciples who didn't walk away from Jesus).
28 These twelve disciples are hardly the ideal candidates for changing the world and announcing the everlasting kingdom. Among them the fishermen Simon Peter and Andrew, James and John, along with Matthew the tax-collector and Judas Iscariot, who will later betray Jesus. Yet choose them as a new Israel, Jesus does.
29 Matt 5:27, Lk 4:22.
30 Mk 11:28, Lk 20:2.
31 Mk 2:7, Lk 5:21, 7:49 (e.g. compare Isa 55:7, Jer 31:35). Assurance of the forgiveness of sins was reserved for the temple and the sacrifices.

Who is this man that even the wind and waves obey him?[32]

Again, this is the question
that preoccupies all four gospels:

Who is this Jesus?

The evangelists assume at the beginnings of their stories that this is the long-awaited Messiah—the Christ, the King. So, in a real way, the reader knows something significant about Jesus from the beginning. This truly is the Anointed One whom Israel has been waiting on. But there are also growing and concerned whispers that Jesus is acting an awful lot like Yahweh.

The gospel of John highlights this theme in a particularly strong way, with his storytelling style story standing out radically from Matthew, Mark and Luke. He's like Vincent van Gogh among renaissance painters—he's painting with completely different strokes. In John, Jesus typically speaks with an extended speech after performing a miraculous sign. Each of these signs point to a deeper reality found in him (living water, true bread, etc.). While the other three gospels depict his unity with Yahweh in their own ways,[33] John's brushstrokes highlight this reality with an unmistakable style.

Who is this man, this rabbi, this Messiah, this Jesus of Nazareth?

Eventually Jesus asks this swelling question to his disciples:

---

[32] Matt 8:27, Mk 4:41, Lk 8:25b (e.g. compare Job 38:8-11, Prov 8:29, Isa 50:2, Jer 31:35). Rhetorical questions like those above show that all of Gospel writers—not just John—take the divinity of Jesus for granted. Questions are asked about Jesus' identity for which the only answer can be "Yahweh."

[33] One example—outside their use of rhetorical questions—can be found in Matt 19:16-30, Mk 10:17-31, Lk 18:18-30: the story of the rich young man. There Jesus answers with a selection from the 10 Words (or 10 Commandments) from Ex 20. In all three, he mentions words #5-9, leaving out the last (dealing with coveting) and the first four (dealing with allegiance to Yahweh). He goes on to tell the man to sell his possessions (addressing #10) and follow him (addressing #1-4). Devotion to Jesus now stands in for devotion to Yahweh.

"Who do people say I am?"[34]

Finally.

Jesus knows that the crowds—and we, the readers—have been asking, so he's finally going to address it. Who is he? The disciples answer with some hesitancy and uncertainty.[35] Word on the street is that he's a reincarnation of the recently executed John the Baptist. Or maybe Elijah has returned? Perhaps even Jeremiah, announcing judgment on the nation again?

But then Jesus turns to the disciples (and us, the readers): *"But what about you?" he asked. "Who do you say I am?"*[36] A decision has to be made. By the disciples and by us too.

Peter famously and boldly answers that Jesus is the Messiah.[37] The Christ. The Anointed One. The "Son of God." The long-anticipated king. The one they've all been waiting for.

Bingo.

Peter is absolutely right, that's definitely who Jesus is. But Peter is also maybe missing something, because Jesus responds in a surprising way —he warns them not to tell anyone.[38]

Jesus is up to something.

There's more to him than they expect.

---

34 Mk 8:27 (see also Matt 16:13 and Lk 9:18. The entire Gospel of John might be considered an extended answer to this question).
35 Matt 16:14, Mk 8:28, Lk 9:19. (Jeremiah is only named in Matthew.)
36 Mk 8:29a (see also Matt 16:15 and Lk 9:20a).
37 Matt 16:16, Mk 8:29b, Lk 9:20b.
38 Matt 16:20, Mk 8:30, Lk 9:21.

All of Israel is watching and waiting for the promises of Yahweh to finally be fulfilled. Their story needs its climax. And the Gospel stories all insist that this climax has arrived in Jesus. He bursts on the scene announcing and enacting the kingdom of God. He's banishing evil and challenging Israel's understanding of the kingdom. He's formed a new Israel around himself. He's definitely the king, but how will he finally establish the kingdom?

Well, Jesus is about to redefine everything: his own identity, the identity of God's people, the nature of Yahweh's kingdom, Yahweh's plan for fulfilling his promises and even the very nature of God himself— everything.

Jesus is about to change the course of human history.

Jesus is going to die.

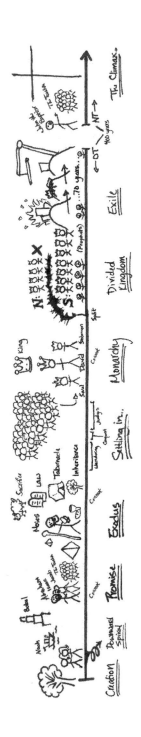

12 climax part two

Israel's story is finally reaching its climax in Jesus. He has begun announcing the long-awaited kingdom of God while he enacts it with his life. Furthermore, he's challenging conventional thinking about Yahweh's rule and reign. Despite their opinions, God's kingdom will not resemble Rome. Israel cannot conjure the kingdom's coming with stricter obedience, stronger rebellion, or sleazy deal-making.

But how, then, will the kingdom come? All the other hopeful "Messiahs" were playing by those rules, but Jesus is not.

The disciples correctly recognize Jesus…
…he is indeed the man who will bring the kingdom.

He is the "Messiah,"
the "Anointed One,"
the "Christ."

He is the King. But what kind of king?

And for that matter, what kind of man is he?

After Peter's great confession, Jesus warns his disciples not to tell anyone and his words take a wildly different, unexpected turn. He begins explaining to his disciples that he must die:

And he said, "The Son of Man must suffer many things and be rejected by the elders, the chief priests and the teachers of the law, and he must be killed and on the third day be raised to life."[1]

Jesus is using the title "Son of Man" for himself. He is tapping into that vision of Daniel 7 that captured the popular imagination of oppressed Israel and fueled their hope for centuries.

He's alluding to an unconquerable, everlasting kingdom.
That's good.

But then he's also talking about his suffering and death.
That's concerning.

But whatever the disciples understood Jesus to mean by this (after all, maybe Jesus is speaking with tricky parables again) they were not taking him literally.[2] After all, this is not the way that a hopeful king should be talking:

The christ should be preparing to vanquish the corrupt religious leaders of Jerusalem. The messiah should be planning how to free both the people and the land from Roman rule.

Jesus should be talking about *conquering*...
...instead he's talking about *being conquered*.

So headstrong Peter takes Jesus aside, perhaps thinking that Jesus needs a lesson in messiahship. He tries to correct him: *"Never, Lord! ...This shall never happen to you!"*[3] But Jesus responds: *"Get*

---

1 Lk 9:22 (see also Matt 16:21 and Mk 8:31).
2 e.g. Mk 8:32 points out that he spoke plainly about this, but they did not understand. Furthermore, Mk 9:10 shows that they are wrestling with what exactly his words about "being raised from the dead" mean.
3 Matt 16:22 (see also Mk 8:33).

behind me, Satan! ...You do not have in mind the concerns of God, but merely human concerns.[4]

Ouch. That one stung.
I think he just called you Satan.

Jesus has no patience for this.

Peter's words are just another form of temptation.

What Jesus is about to do—and how he is going to do it—will look profoundly different than all the "human concerns" which have preoccupied Israel for the last several centuries. Jesus has his eyes on a bigger kingdom than merely Israel, and he has his will set against a bigger enemy than merely Rome.

Jesus will not back down from his strange path—the path toward suffering and death. Nor does he limit this suffering to himself. The path he has set for himself is the path his disciples must follow:

"Whoever wants to be my disciple must deny themselves and take up their cross daily and follow me."[5]

These words absolutely perplex his disciples.

It was bad enough that Jesus was talking about dying, but now he's telling them to take up their... crosses? Crucifixion is what happens when Rome squashes a rebellion. Crucifixion is what happens when a Messiah fails. The disciples are trying to talk to Jesus about the grand promises of

4 Mk 8:33b (see also Matt 16:25).
5 Luke 8:23b (see also Matt 16:24 & Mk 8:34b).

Yahweh being fulfilled, but Jesus keeps bringing up suffering and death. Both his and theirs.

And yet in the very same breath, he also tells them that the kingdom promised in Daniel 7 will be established within their lifetimes.[6]

"Alright," they must have thought, "we'll see how this plays out."

Perhaps Jesus is still speaking in riddles.

Because kingdom and crucifixion are incompatible.

Not long after starting this shocking death-talk, Jesus climbs to the top of a mountain along with three of his closest disciples—Peter, James and John. When they arrive at the top, the scene becomes surreal and strange.

Jesus is "transfigured" in front of them. Not something you see everyday. Instead of their dusty rabbi, these disciples are suddenly staring at a dazzling and radiant figure. On each side of him are two symbols of Israel's story, Moses and Elijah. The ancient lawgiver and the iconic prophet. The heavenly voice from Jesus' baptism returns here: Jesus is Yahweh's king and anointed servant—the disciples must listen to him.[7]

The Jewish people have been waiting over a millennium for a prophet like Moses to be raised up.[8] Now the divine voice adds Deuteronomy's words to his baptism's royal coronation. Heaven is implying that the

---

6 Matt 16:28, Mk 9:1, Lk 19:27.

7 Matt 17:1-9, Mk 9:2-10, Lk 9:28-36 The account of the transfiguration does not appear in John's gospel. I heard it once said that John's entire gospel is a kind of transfiguration, to which I respond, "fair enough."

8 The promise of one like Moses is found in Deut 18:15-18 and watching for him is found in Deut 34:10-12. N.T. Wright, *Matthew for Everyone, Part 2* (Louisville, KY: WJK Press, 2004), 15.

Prophet is finally here.[9] So listen closely, even if some of what he's saying doesn't make sense right now.

And then suddenly Jesus is alone. Moses, Elijah, majestic cloud, glorious light—all gone. Only their dusty rabbi approaching and saying, *"Don't be afraid."*[10]

Listen to him.

The disciples will definitely need to heed Jesus' words and hold them tightly. Because Jesus is about to lead them into the heart of darkness.

We—the readers—are becoming more and more convinced that Jesus is setting himself on a course that will ultimately lead to his death. He seems serious—he tells his disciples two more times that he is going to suffer and die.[11]

They still do not understand. How could they? What Jesus is saying does not make any sense. The Messiah they expected—by definition—does not suffer and die. He conquers and establishes the kingdom.

A dead king is no king at all.

Luke frames this section of his Gospel with Jesus willfully setting out for Jerusalem.[12] His reason for heading there? *"Because it is impossible that a prophet should be killed outside Jerusalem."*[13]

---

9 For example, notice the way "the Prophet" is talked about in Jn 1:21, 1:25, 6:14, 7:40. This anticipation is rooted in Deut 18:15, 18.
10 Matt 17:7b.
11 Second time: Matt 17:22-23, Mk 9:30-37, Lk 9:43-45. Third time: Matt 20:17-19, Mk 10:32-34, Lk 18:31-34.
12 Lk 9:51. See also 9:53, 13:22, 17:11, 18:31, 19:28.
13 Lk 13:33b.

Jesus is not a victim.
He knows exactly what he's doing.

And evidently he knows that he *must* do it.

As he heads to Jerusalem, Jesus continues to teach about the kingdom. According to Jesus, life under the rule of Yahweh looks nothing like Israel expected. Everything is upside down:

The wealthy, self-sufficient are poor while the desperate are rich. [14]

Real power looks like serving [15]
instead of Alexander the Great.

The greatest in the kingdom are those who are least. [16]

Grace and forgiveness are dished out in embarrassing excess. [17]

Those who lose their lives
are those who will live. [18]

The King rides a peaceful donkey instead of a war stallion. [19]

That's precisely the way that Jesus chooses to enter Jerusalem when he arrives there. Neither Matthew nor John want you to miss the implications:

---

[14] Mk 10:17-27 (Matt 19:16-26 & Lk 19:18-27). We might note that the story of Zacchaeus in Luke 19:1-10 shows the impossible possibility that Jesus spoke of in Lk 18:27 and parallels.
[15] Mk 10:35-45 (Matt 20:20-28) and Jn 13:1-17.
[16] Matt 11:11 & Lk 7:28, 9:48.
[17] Matt 6:14-15, 18:21-35; Mk 11:25; Lk 6:37, 17:3, 23:34.
[18] Matt 16:25, Mk 8:35, Lk 9:24.
[19] Matt 21:1-11, Mk 11:1-10, Lk 19:28-40; Jn 12:12-15.

Yahweh would ride into Jerusalem on a donkey as King.[20]

Now Jesus is riding into Jerusalem on a donkey.

And as Jesus approaches Jerusalem, he weeps over it.[21] Neither the Jewish people nor Jerusalem recognize what is happening. Yahweh is finally coming to this city in the most surprising of ways. And he's weeping of all things! He knows that his people and their city have chosen to compete with the beastly kingdoms on their own beastly terms —and it's going to destroy them in just a few short decades.[22]

For centuries, Yahweh confronted religious corruption, hypocrisy and injustice through the prophets. Now he himself has become the Prophet. Jesus enters Jerusalem, preparing to confront the corruption and darkness which has eaten its way into the heart of Israel. The corrupt leaders of Israel historically hated the prophets, and the religious establishment in Jesus' day will do the same. They have no patience for this backwoods Galilean confronting them with truth.

Once in Jerusalem, Jesus enters the temple—Yahweh's temple.

Let that sink in…. the glorious presence of Yahweh has returned to the temple. But in the most humble and unlikely of ways.

In the temple, Jesus enacts a grand protest that ever-so-briefly shuts down the sacrificial system.[23] The prophet Jeremiah had once called

20 Matt 21:4-5 and Jn 12:15 referencing Zech 9:9 (see also 14:9).
21 Lk 19:41.
22 The Roman general Titus destroys Jerusalem and the temple in 70 AD because of Jewish rebellion against Rome—their trying to establish Yahweh's kingdom on their own terms. Jesus anticipates this and agonizes over their rebellion, their rejection of him and their refusal of the way of peace in Lk 19:42-44.
23 Matt 21:12-17; Mk 11:12-21; Lk 19:45-48. John frames Jesus' ministry by placing this incident at the beginning of his ministry in 2:13-25, as if to set the stage for what Jesus' career is about. (Some scholars, however, dispute this "creative license" by John and think John's account is a separate temple cleansing.)

Solomon's temple *"a den of robbers,"* and now Jesus repeats those words to decry a similar corruption of his day.[24] These people have become obsessed with Israel as a nation—obsessed with Israel *above* the nations.

But in the same breath, Jesus also speaks the hope-filled promises of Isaiah: *"my house will be called a house of prayer for all nations."*[25] Unlike those around him, he remembers that the promises of Yahweh were always about Israel *for* the nations. Hopeful that the outsiders would become insiders.

They were blessed to be a blessing.

Over the next few days, the religious leaders challenge Jesus in the courts of the temple. His growing popularity threatens their positions and power, so they send wave after wave of questions crashing over him.[26] Maybe they can trip him up. But alas, he deflects and diffuses all their questions—often succeeding in publicly exposing what an embarrassing, two-faced group they really are.

And then he tells them another parable.

Afterward, they storm away, dizzy with anger. They can't really remember all the specifics of it. It was something about a vineyard that was entrusted to a group of people. Yes, that was it! The vineyard was their responsibility. But those people eventually began to think themselves special, seizing the vineyard as a selfish privilege to exploit. They ignored, mistreated and killed the owner's servants and finally even killed

24 Matt 21:13, Mk 11:17, Lk 19:46 quoting Jer 7:11.
25 The phrase "for all the nations" is included in Mk 11:17 but omitted from both Matt 21:13 and Lk 19:46.
26 Mk 11:27-12:40 (Matt 21:23-22:46 & Lk 20).

the landowner's very own son. And so the landowner is giving the vineyard to others—to those who will humbly serve him and bear fruit.[27]

This rabbi from Nazareth has gone too far! They got the gist of what he was saying! Yahweh might give Israel's privileges to others!?

They've got to do something to stop this man—

He's bordering blasphemy!
He's trumpeting treason!

They walk away and begin searching for a way and time to arrest him.[28] It will be tricky though. Jesus is incredibly popular and he has come to Jerusalem during an incredibly symbolic week. This is the week where hundreds of thousands of Jews flock to Jerusalem and when revolution spreads like wildfire. It celebrates past and future liberation from foreign oppressors. It unnerves local Roman officials and makes them trigger-happy.

This is the week of the Passover festival.

And it makes quite a symbolic stage.

Jesus and his disciples find a host home with an upper room where they can celebrate this ancient and sacred meal. But as they eat and celebrate, Jesus startles his disciples again. Specific words were traditionally spoken during that meal—words to remember their exodus from Egypt. These words had been spoken by thousands for centuries.[29]

27 Matt 21:33-44; Mk 12:1-11; Lk 20:9-18.
28 Matt 21:45-46; Mk 12:12; Lk 20:19.
29 Alfred Edersheim, The Life and Times of Jesus the Messiah (Peabody, MA: Hendrickson, 1993), 817.

But instead of talking about the "bread of affliction," he talks about his body broken for them.[30] Instead of thanking Yahweh for the fruit of the vine, he lifts the cup and calls it his blood—the new covenant in his blood.[31]

Excuse me, Jesus?
The new covenant?

As in the new covenant promised by the prophets?[32]

Yahweh had rescued his people from Egypt and established a covenant with them at Sinai. That's what this meal has always been about. But Jesus is talking about something new. He's talking about a rescue being enacted and a covenant being established right now—*by him* and *in him.*

Either this is incredibly self-deluded heresy or something marvelous is happening. What if Yahweh is fulfilling his promises in a way no one ever imagined?

And in the flesh no less.

After eating this bizarre Passover meal with his disciples, Jesus goes out to the Mount of Olives near Jerusalem to pray. And his prayer is absolute agony. There's "a cup" that he'd prefer to pass on.[33] Quite understandably, he doesn't want to drink the dregs of Yahweh's wrath.[34] But he'll do it if that's what his Father wants.

To the last drop.

---

30 Matt 26:26, Mk 14:22, Lk 22:19 (compare with "bread of affliction" in Deut 16:3).

31 Matt 26:27-28, Mk 14:24, Lk 22:20 (compare with Ex 24:8).

32 e.g. Jer 31:31-34 (also Ezk 16:59-63).

33 Mk 14:34-36 (Matt 26:38-42 & Lk 22:42-44).

34 The "cup of wrath" is a common image found in Israel's prophecies. Yahweh, as a God of justice, will pour out his wrath on those who continue in rebellion, be it the nations or Israel itself. (e.g. Isa 51:17-23, Jer 25:15-29, Ezk 23:31-34).

Jesus is in agony; his disciples are asleep.

The new Israel isn't any more reliable than the old one.

Jesus will have to be faithful for all of them.

One of his inner circle—one of the Twelve—arrives. Judas Iscariot has betrayed him. He's got an armed escort with him. With a kiss, he marks Jesus as the man to arrest. A handful of disciples want to fight, but Jesus forbids it.[35]

He chose to come to Jerusalem. He is not a victim here.
He will not contribute to any kind of cycle of violence.

The violence stops with him—on him.

The Jewish leaders orchestrate a series of trials throughout the night,[36] hustling Jesus from building to building, down this street and down that alley. A decision must be made about this man. He stands before the Jewish council, before the regional king (named Herod) and twice before the Roman governor (named Pontius Pilate). As the night continues, the situation deteriorates with the foreign soldiers and local religious powers growing more bold and more aggressive.

They mock him and strip him naked.
They beat him and dress him in costumes.

Night gives way to morning, and his accusers all reach differing conclusions. The Jewish leadership believes him to be a heretic threatening their theology and power. Herod dismisses him as a mildly

---

35 Mk 14:43-50 (Matt 26:47-56, Lk 22:47-53, Jn 18:1-14).
36 Matt 26:57-68, 27:11-31; Mk 14:53-65, 15:1-20; Lk 22:63-23:25; Jn 18:19-40, 19:1-16. The trial before Herod is only recorded in Luke.

amusing curiosity. Pilate seriously doubts the Jewish leaders' charges that Jesus is a rebel insurgent plotting an overthrow of Rome. But, then again, he's also anxious about a horde of people breaking into a riot—or worse, full rebellion!—on his watch. This Jewish people has a history of rebellion.

So he pulls the trigger.

Pilate will crucify Jesus if that's what they really want.

The passion narrative of Jesus has been told and retold through the centuries and nothing new can be said here. The Romans had perfected execution into a horrifying art form they could put on display to prevent future rebellions.

Blood and bruising.
Sweat and swelling.
Throbbing and stinging.

Crucifixion, dehydration, asphyxiation and death.[37]

"My God, my God, why have you forsaken me?"[38]

The corrupted religion of Israel and the brutal power of Rome join hands to kill "the King of the Jews."[39] The nations of the world join the kingdom of priests to execute Yahweh.

And he allows it.

---

[37] Matt 27:32-56, Mk 15:21-41, Lk 23:26-49; Jn 19:16-37.

[38] Matt 27:46, Mk 15:34. Jesus is quoting the beginning of Ps 22 which, as a psalm, captures the heart of his suffering and later vindication. Also noteworthy is the echo of Deut 31:17 that Jesus seems to be enduring on behalf of Israel (and the world).

[39] The ironic sign placed on the top of the cross ("King of the Jews") is recorded in all four gospels: Matt 27:37, Mk 15:26, Lk 23:38, Jn 19:19-22.

The nightmare of creation's downward spiral has hit its lowest point. Darkness covers the land as history reaches its blackest moment— Jesus of Nazareth dies.

The King has been crucified.

We well know, of course, that the story does not end here. But that knowledge means that all of the suspense, surprise, and irony is almost entirely lost upon us.

According to everyone's experience—

to the laws of biology—
to first-century Jewish theology—
to the disciples own expectations—
to all common sense—

Jesus should have stayed dead.

No one—especially not his disciples—expected anything different.

A dead king is no king at all.

Game over.

He played chicken with the system and the system won.

Darkness, despair, and death
hold all the power in this world.

But God is full of surprises.

As our story begins, he sees utter nothingness and says,
"Not so fast. Enough of this darkness, let there be light."
As humanity rebels and spirals downward, he says,
"Not so fast. I will bless all the world through Abraham."
As Israel screams under the whips of Egypt, he says,
"Not so fast. I have heard your cries, and I will rescue you."
As years of exile drive Israel to the brink of despair, he says,
"Not so fast. I will recreate you—and all the world too."
And as Jesus of Nazareth lies cold and dead, he says,
"Not so fast. The darkness will not overcome the light."

It's the third day that Jesus has been dead. Women who knew him come to his tomb, planning to anoint his corpse with spices. All has been lost—he wasn't the messiah of Israel after all. But he was still a dear mentor. A leader. A friend. A great man. They can honor him in this small way.

They don't know that this is a different sort of day.

Easter.

They arrive at the tomb and receive shocking news from heavenly messengers: Jesus has been resurrected. He's not dead. He is alive. Long and short of it—he's not there. I mean, he definitely was there—dead and decaying in the tomb—but now he's not.

Did you feel that?

A worldview just shifted. The resurrection that the Jewish people anticipated happening on history's *last day* has invaded *this day*.[40] New

---

Creation has finally arrived. In person. And he's smiling through his scars.

Jesus appears to his disciples with the world's most glorious, hilarious, and haunting "I told you so."

Those who are willing receive restored relationship.[41] Jesus knew what he was talking about—it wasn't a riddle at all. He proved himself trustworthy. He recounts their long history—the story of Israel—and insists: "That's all been about me."[42]

And now the disciples are charged to go and tell others what they've seen, what they've heard and what they know.[43] To tell the Story that all humanity never realized they were living.

Tell them so they can know
of God's faithfulness in Jesus.

Tell them so they can embrace it.
Tell them so they can obey it.

Tell them so they can repent.
Tell them so they reject death.

Tell them so they can worship.
Tell them so they can choose life.

The disciples simply must tell this story. Because this isn't merely a feel-good, campfire story. This is a life-changing, society-shaping, world-

41 Contrast the different responses of Peter (Jn 21:15-17) and Judas (Matt 27:1-5) after their betrayals.
42 Lk 24:27, 44.
43 Matt 28:18-20, Lk 24:48. (1 Cor 15:1-8 and 1 Jn 1:1 are emphatic that this was something they experienced in history.)

transforming, darkness-breaking Story. It's the true Story of Creation being stitched back together by its Creator being torn apart. And it's the story that mercifully demands both communities and individuals to take up their crosses and follow the crucified and resurrected King.

Because embracing the cross is how he conquers.

Crucifixion and resurrection
is what the kingdom looks like.

That's how it spreads.
That's where life is found.

Jesus spends forty days with his disciples before he is taken from their sight in a cloud.[44] The disciples watch Daniel 7 unfold before their very eyes—the Son of Man ascends to the Ancient of Days and receives an everlasting kingdom that will never be destroyed.[45]

There is glorious good news to embrace and announce:

"God has made this Jesus, whom you crucified,
both Lord and Messiah."[46]

Israel's story and human history have reached their climax.

Long live the King.

---

[44] Lk 24:51, Acts 1:9.
[45] Compare Daniel 7:13-14 with the above (and also Matt 16:28, Mk 9:1, Lk 19:27). Thanks to N.T. Wright, *Acts for Everyone, Part 1,* 13-14 (Louisville, KY: WJK Press, 2008) for recognizing this.
[46] Acts 2:36b.

Part Two

LIVING IN THE STORY OF JESUS
(A.K.A. ACTS TO REVELATION)

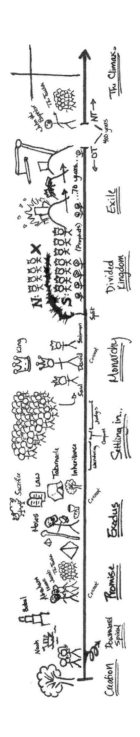

Creation

Downward Spiral

Promise

Exodus

Settling in...

Monarchy

Divided Kingdom

Exile

The Climax

13 king of the universe

In the beginning God was King. His royal song brought all of creation dancing into existence. It was good, it was good, it was very good. Until it wasn't. Until his subjects rebelled against his reign, plunging the goodness of his kingdom under the dominion of death.

His subjects scorned and hated him.
Death ruled as a twisted tyrant in his place.

But the King remained faithful.

Humanity's rejected King began the slow, quiet work of reclaiming the throne through a small family. His kingdom, now cursed with thorns and thistles, would once again be blessed. His rebellious subjects—now terrorized by death—would once again have their rightful King reigning forever. The tyrant on the throne would be vanquished; death would die. Creation would again be blessed.

All of Israel's story anticipated the return of the King.

It's no surprise, then, that we find Jesus' disciples asking their resurrected Rabbi about this kingdom. His resurrection, after all, vindicated him, proving him to really be God's Anointed One. So what will his reign look like?[1]

---

1 Acts 1:6

This coming kingdom was critical to their worldview. Yahweh had tied his promise to bless the world with a promise of a king—even from the very earliest parts of Israel's story. From the start, God's promise to bless the world assumed that a king would eventually come from Abraham.[2] This family's royalty destiny was proclaimed even before Genesis ended. After he settled in Egypt, Jacob spoke blessings over his twelve sons with his dying breaths and proclaimed:

"The scepter will not depart from Judah, nor the ruler's staff from between his feet, until he to whom it belongs shall come and the obedience of the nations shall be his."[3]

David had been from the tribe of Judah, but this promise was always bigger than the son of Jesse. David gave us a faint shadow of what God's kingship would be like. But eventually even David died.

Like every other king.
Like every other man.

Yahweh had promised that an everlasting kingdom was coming.[4]

A king to rule the nations
would come from the tribe of Judah.

Blessing would flood the world through Abraham's royal family.

As we've already seen, anticipation built through the Old Testament as Israel watched all kinds of other kings—Assyrian, Babylonian, Persian, Macedonian and eventually Roman—rise and fall on the world stage. It

2 Gen 17:6-7 (king) is planted right in the middle of 12:2-3, 18:18, 22:17-18 (world-wide blessing).
3 Gen 49:10.
4 2 Sam 7:11-16 (see also Ps 18:50, 89:3-4, 132:10-18; Jer 23:5-6, 33:14-17; Ezk 34:23-24, 37:24-25, Zech 13:1).

seemed they were always being ruled by a foreign king, even while writings like Daniel stirred their imaginations to remember Yahweh's coming kingdom.[5]

But when will it finally happen? That was the gnawing question. When will the King of the Jews finally appear?

The four gospels all give the same answer—right now.

We can often miss the evangelists announcing the kingship of Jesus for two reasons. First, we may assume the Bible's message ("the Gospel") is about something else and may be hunting for that. Or second, we ignore the Bible's elegance and art, assuming it's not making a point unless it's coarsely blunt.

Take Luke's gospel as an example of this cunning artistry—he fills his telling of Jesus' life with nods and winks that Jesus is the true King. As he begins his account, he frames John the Baptist's birth with strong echoes of an early story:

The priest in the temple, the promise of a son to a barren mother, the celebratory songs—it all sounds a lot like Samuel's birth.[6] It's subtle and genius. John the Baptizer is the new Samuel, and this new Samuel will anoint the new David.

It's certainly no coincidence that Luke includes the name of the angel announcing all of this—Gabriel.[7] Wasn't that the name of the angel who appeared in Daniel, promising that the kingdom would soon appear?[8]

---

5 e.g. Dan 2 & 7 (see 2:44 and 7:13-14).
6 Compare Lk 1:5-25, 39-45, 57-80 with 1 Sam 1:1-2:11, see N.T. Wright, The New Testament and the People of God, 379-381.
7 Lk 1:19, 26-27.
8 Dan 8:16, 9:21.

Now here in Luke, the true King is finally taking the throne![9] These are Gabriel's only two appearances in the Bible, and in both he announces God's kingdom.

The reign of Israel's God—the good Creator—is so close!

No wonder Luke recounts Jesus' uncle and mother singing of holy revolution in response to this news.[10] There are so many others who seemed to be in charge—the regional king (Herod[11]), the governor (Quirinius) and the emperor of Rome himself (Caesar Augustus).[12] The entire time that Jesus proclaims and enacts Yahweh's reign, these figures loom large in the background.

Israel has been used to many other kings on many other thrones.

Jesus is later arrested and put on trial by these "powerful" figures. But a great irony actually emerges. The gospel-writers understand Jesus to be the true King and he's standing before various rulers who think themselves in charge. And to our surprise, Jesus allows these beastly rulers—Herod, Pilate and even Israel's own religious leaders—to put him on trial as a heretical revolutionary and even to execute him.[13]

For centuries Israel had felt trampled and torn apart by the nations. Now their true King, the Son of Man, has come and endured exactly that.[14] The King allowed himself to be crucified.[15]

---

9 Lk 1:30-33.
10 Lk 1:46-55 & 2:67-79. These are overtly political and practical in talking about God's coming reign.
11 We might note that "Herod" can refer to different members of the same family who succeed each other (Herod the Great, Herod Agrippa, Herod Antipas).
12 Lk 1:5, 2:1-2.
13 Notice the charges leveled against Jesus (and his response!) in Lk 23:1-3.
14 Dan 7:15-27.
15 A reminder of Jesus' kingship while he is on the cross is given by all four gospels: Matt 27:37, Mk 15:26, Lk 23:38, Jn 19:19-22.

But now here he stands. The disciples are standing in front of him, asking him about the kingdom and his kingship. Because he didn't stay dead. Because his resurrection proved that the beastly kingdoms do not have final authority. And neither do their self-deluded, self-appointed kings. Neither does the curse whose thorns crowned Jesus as he died.[16]

No, the slain Lamb sits on the throne—he has final authority.[17]

The Son of Man has finally shown himself to be King.[18]

Life, light, and love have the final authority.

Jesus threw himself headlong
into the jaws of all other authorities
so that they would choke on him.[19]

The light shines in the darkness,
and the darkness has not overcome it.[20]

Death has been swallowed up in victory.[21]
His kingdom will never end.[22]

The supreme kingship of Jesus is the center of the message that the earliest disciples declared:

---

16 Mk 15:17 (Matt 27:29, Jn 19:2-5), Gen 3:18.

17 Rev 5:6-10.

18 The point of the ascension (Lk 24:51, Acts 1:9) and the frequently repeated image of Jesus sitting at God's right hand (see Ps 110; Matt 22:41-46, 26:64; Mk 12:35-37, 14:62; Lk 20:41-44, 22:69; Acts 2:33, 7:55; Rom 8:34; Eph 1:20; Col 3:1; Heb 1:3, 8:1, 10:12, 12:2; 1 Pet 3:22) is that Jesus in all his full humanity is now already King over all the universe. The human race has a fully human (and fully divine) King who will one day lay all of his kingdom under the rule of God (1 Cor 15:27-28).

19 Col 2:15.

20 Jn 1:5.

21 1 Cor 15:54b (alluding to Isa 25:7-8)

22 Lk 1:33b (alluding to 2 Sam 7:11-16).

Here is a King whom even death cannot hold.[23]

Jesus is Lord.[24]

And THAT is the incredibly good news—that's **the gospel.**

We've become so accustomed to it that it's hard to appreciate its radical double significance—how politically dangerous it was in Rome and how religiously heretical it was in Judaism:

First, the disciples of Jesus were making the dangerous claim that Caesar was not the king of the world. This made them enemies of the state—their ultimate allegiance lay elsewhere. After all, there really is a King running the universe, and he demands (and deserves!) our absolute allegiance.

Second, the disciples called Jesus "Lord," which would have sounded like heresy to Jews—in fact, most of them were Jews! But "Lord" (kurios) was the way the Greek translation of the Old Testament referred to Yahweh.[25] Furthermore Yahweh alone is Israel's true King.[26] And now Jesus is being called not only "King" but also "Lord."[27] The allegiance of these Christians lay not to stale religious traditions about Yahweh but to Yahweh himself.

They were proclaiming that Jesus is Yahweh made known to us.[28]

---

23 Acts 2:24-36.
24 e.g. Acts 28:31, Rom 10:9, 1 Cor 12:3.
25 The translated Greek title "kurios" ("Lord") was placed into the Greek translation of the Old Testament as a substitute for Yahweh in the same way that "LORD" is in most English translations. Both "kurios" and "LORD" are titles of respect and reverence substituting for the name too holy to say. That "too holy name" ends up becoming synonymous with Jesus.
26 e.g. Psalm 47; Isa 33:22, 52:7.
27 e.g. Compare the climactic Phil 2:10-11 (and Rom 14:11-12) with Isa 45:23. Also compare 1 Cor 8:6 with Deut 6:4, and Ps 145:10-13.
28 Jn 1:18, 2 Cor 4:4b, Col 1:15, Heb 1:3.

That Yahweh has become known and celebrated as King in Jesus.

Jesus is Lord.
King of the universe.

All of society, popular culture and conventional wisdom seems to proclaim, "Caesar is Lord!"[29] But the disciples' message was that there is another king—the real King.[30] And his resurrection from the dead proves that he is worthy of loyalty and devotion.[31] Giving him allegiance means being out of the dominion of darkness and into light—into life and forgiveness and freedom.[32]

And the scandal of all this is that it's true.

Jesus really did die.
He really did resurrect.
He really does reign.

Loyalty to the reality of Jesus' reign meant his earliest followers had to live radically different from the (political, religious, social, etc) cultures around them. Their loyalty belonged to the King of the universe who established his power through self-sacrificial love. And it demanded they act accordingly.

When Paul says that our *citizenship is in heaven*,[33] he does not mean to imply that we're waiting around for the day when we can finally go to that place where the kingdom already is. Rather he's borrowing from the

---

29 This was a common propaganda slogan of the day for Rome (N.T. Wright, *What Saint Paul Really Said*, 88.) Though Rome's slogan does not appear in the New Testament, the counter-claim about Jesus certainly does.
30 Acts 17:7 (contrast with Jn 19:12-15).
31 Acts 2:32-39.
32 Col 1:12-14.
33 Phil 3:20a. See 20b-21—we await a "Savior *from* there" who will transform reality *here* (see also Col 3:1-4 and Rev 21:1-4). Philippi, as a Roman colony, would be very aware of the way colonies work.

language of Roman colonies. Colonies were communities who established the language, culture, and presence of Rome in a particular place. Paul's understanding was that we—as citizens of heaven—are to establish colonies of heaven here and now. Colonies reflecting the reality of our King here and now.

C.S. Lewis wrote, "Christianity is the story of how the rightful King has landed, you might say in disguise, and is calling us all to take part in His great campaign of sabotage."[34]

Christians are the saboteurs of death.
Christians are the colonists of heaven.

We are to announce the Lordship of Jesus, bend our hearts to his reign and devote our loyalty to his kingdom.

We are to strive to live in harmony with how the universe was meant to be. To sacrifice for the good of others. To live in harmony with the beat of our living King's heart.[35]

We are to pray for his reign to be made known on earth as it is in heaven.[36] This is one of our central—and most neglected—tasks in the world. It's so central because only our King can establish his kingdom. And it's neglected because it deals an unbearable blow to our pride. We must confess (over and over) that Jesus' kingdom can only be established by his work—and ultimately by his return.

---

[34] C.S. Lewis, *Mere Christianity* (New York: Harper Collins, 2001), 46.
[35] This is why you find the early Christians living as such a tight, supportive prayer-centered community in the early part of Acts (2:42-47, 4:32-35). They're trying to embody the loving, self-sacrificial reign of Jesus as a community.
[36] Matt 6:9-13, Lk 11:2-4.

So we announce the kingdom, we enact the kingdom and we pray for the kingdom. King Jesus[37] announced, enacted, and prayed for the kingdom, and we are charged to do the same.[38]

This means us asking, among other things:
"What does the redemptive reign of Jesus look like here?"

Over anything.
Over everything.

There are some kingdoms that are so beastly—so rooted in dehumanizing selfishness, exploitation and violence—that they simply cannot be redeemed.[39] Kingdoms that crucify. The reign of Jesus over these (dare we call them "demonic"?) kingdoms must mean that he destroys them.

What else could a good King do?

But the Creator's vast creation is good at its core. So the "kingdoms" of economies and education, politics and pop culture, mathematics and metaphysics, arts and agriculture—all of them are good at their core. Colonists of heaven announce, enact and pray for the reign of Jesus over all these spheres of life.

We want every bit of creation to be brought under the life-giving reign of Jesus. One theologian said, "There is not a square inch in the whole domain of our human existence over which Christ, who is Sovereign over *all*, does not cry: 'Mine!'"[40]

---

[37] Another fine translation of "Christ Jesus," by the way.
[38] e.g. Matt 28:18-20.
[39] e.g. Rev 18:21-24, 21:7-8. Examples of these dehumanizing "kingdoms" include drug trade, pornography, human trafficking, arms dealing, etc.
[40] Abraham Kuyper, "Sphere Sovereignty," in Abraham Kuyper: A Centennial Reader, ed. James D. Bratt (Grand Rapids: Eerdmans, 1998), 488.

So churches do not need more "professional ministers." Rather, churches need to recognize that they are weekly gatherings of colonists loyal to the Kingdom. Colonists of heaven who enact love,[41] justice,[42] equality,[43] generosity,[44] and every other creative goodness[45] in all the different spheres of life. The church cannot afford to pretend like Sunday mornings are the pinnacle of worship or the kingdom.

Jesus is King over all...
...even if it looks like Saul is still king.

And the King's colonists prayerfully claim every bit of it for him.

And a word of caution: this does not mean that "the church" (as an organization) should be trying to strong-arm or control these different spheres. Periods of church history (particularly in late Rome and medieval Europe) saw the church trying to do just that. This hardly reflects our King's patience throughout history, his emptying himself of power or his self-sacrificing love. The church is to announce, enact and pray with the knowledge that the fullness of the kingdom will arrive with the return of Jesus.[46]

The church is not the King.
The church is the King's bride.

And she cannot sit on his throne—she can only prepare it.

---

41 e.g. Rom 13:9-10, Gal 5:14, Ja 2:8.
42 e.g. Acts 6:1-7, Ja 1:27.
43 e.g. Gal 3:28, Eph 6:5-9, Col 3:11, Philemon 15-16.
44 e.g. Acts 2:42-47, Rom 15:27, 2 Cor 9:6-15, 1 Tim 6:18-19.
45 e.g. Eph 2:10, Titus 3:1, 8; Heb 10:24-25.
46 Acts 1:10.

And one day God *will* decisively act to bring his rule and reign to earth *fully*.[47] This True David—who really is already the King—will finally be recognized. The entire universe will indeed be a particular way in the end —it will be good, it will be good, it will be very good. It will reflect the good Creator's heart. The various "kingdoms" of this world will fully give way to the kingdom of Jesus.[48]

And *the last enemy to be destroyed is death*.[49]

Jesus is King.
Jesus is Lord.

This is incredibly good news.

One day he will be revealed and his kingdom fully established. Until then, Christians are colonists of heaven claiming every bit of creation through self-sacrificing love on behalf of our King.

Because God has revealed his heart, and that's what it looks like.

That's why the supreme kingship of anyone can be good news.

Because of his heart.
Because of his self-sacrificing love.

---

47 Isa 65:17-25, Rev 21:1-4.
48 1 Cor 15:24-25, Rev 11:15.
49 1 Cor 15:26.

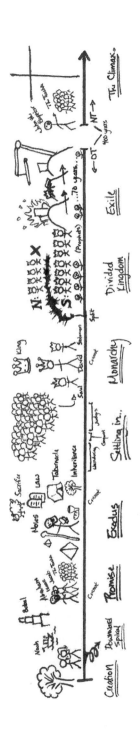

14 the final sacrifice

The death of Jesus was no accident. The New Testament will simply not allow us to understand the cross as a catastrophe that cuts short the otherwise promising career of Jesus.

No, Jesus is the King who chose a cross.
But why? Why choose the cross?

The bloody end of Jesus' life has become so familiar to us—we've become so calloused to the cross—that we can't process how shocking and strange it was. But however unexpected the cross first was, it became crucial to the first disciples. After watching Jesus ascend into heaven, they spent the rest of their lives proclaiming not simply that Jesus was alive, and not simply that Jesus was Lord, but also that Jesus had been crucified.[1]

One of the earliest Christian leaders, Paul of Tarsus, insisted that the crucifixion of Jesus had become the center of how he understood the universe: *For I resolved to know nothing while I was with you except Jesus Christ and him crucified.*[2]

A shameful Roman execution stake has become the lens through which Paul sees all reality? Really?

---

[1] Notice how in the early sermons of Acts, the cross is talked about as "God's deliberate plan" (2:23) and repeatedly linked with salvation (2:36-38, 3:18-19, 4:10-12, 5:30-31, 10:39-43).
[2] 1 Cor 2:2.

Indeed it has, answers Paul. He declares Jesus' cross to be the deepest wisdom of God that destroys all conventional thinking, challenging all our assumptions about true justice, true wisdom and true life.[3] And for two thousand years, the church has joined with Paul in boasting about the "foolishness" of Jesus' death.

You see, the earliest Christians understood their King's death to be a sacrifice. An entirely different sacrifice than anything the world ever knew. It was the sacrifice to end all sacrifices.

The final sacrifice.

Sacrifices appear early and often starting in Genesis. Cain and Abel instinctually make sacrifices to Yahweh right after the exile from Eden.[4] They know that something needs to be done to repair their relationship with the divine. A few chapters later we found Yahweh stopping Abraham from carrying out the sacrifice of Isaac. He is not a God who approves of sacrificing children.[5]

He is a God who provides the sacrifice himself.

Turn the pages. At Sinai, Yahweh gives the Israelites a detailed sacrificial system, reminding them of their need for forgiveness and his willingness to graciously give it.[6] The ancient world ate, drank and breathed sacrifice.

Israel knew all about sacrifice.

---

[3] 1 Cor 1:22-24.
[4] Gen 4:1-12.
[5] Gen 22:1-19 (see also Lev 18:21, Jer 19:5).
[6] e.g. Lev 1-7, 16.

Turn the pages and—lo and behold—here come the prophets! And they condemned sacrifices as bankrupt, hypocritical rituals when done by rebellious, corrupt people.[7] Insincere people have worn religion as a mask for thousands of years, and Yahweh was never interested in the blood or flesh of animals.[8]

He was interested in their hearts.[9]

Sacrifices could not take away sin—they could remind Israel that they needed Yahweh to cleanse them.[10] They could only remind people that wholeness and forgiveness and restoration lay outside of themselves. And the sacrifices became pointless, meaningless distractions if the slaughtered animals weren't driving people to their knees and compelling them to lives defined by goodness, justice and gratitude.

Turn the pages, and we've arrived at Jesus again.

He came, he saw, he died—he conquered by being conquered.

Then he wadded up death
and tossed it in the clothes hamper.

He won't be wearing that again.

And after his resurrection, the followers of Jesus saw everything in a new light. The death of Jesus became something loaded with profound weight and significance. The author of Hebrews, for example, devotes large lengths of his sermon[11] to recall both Israel's history and sacrificial

---

7 e.g. 1 Sam 15:22, Isa 1:11-17, Hosea 6:6, Amos 5:21-27, Micah 6:6-8.

8 e.g. Ps 50:7-15.

9 Micah 6:6-8

10 Heb 10:3-4.

11 That's essentially what the book of **Hebrews** is—a sermon to Jewish Christians who may be tempted to disguise their faith in Jesus as Judaism to avoid persecution by local communities and by Rome.

system. It all pointed to something. All the nitty-gritty details of the sacrificial system—the various sacrifices, the high priest, the sprinkled blood, the Day of Atonement, all of them—were shadows of something.

Shadows of the King; shadows of Jesus.[12]

All of Israel's sacrifices anticipated a day when Yahweh would finally deal once and for all with the rebellion, corruption and darkness of Israel, as well as the rest of creation. Sacrifice had long promised "forgiveness" to rebels, "purification" to the corrupt, and "light" to the darkened. Creation needed all of the above.

Sacrifices soberly reminded us of these needs.
And sacrifices reminded us that God gives freely.

We needed plenty of reminding because creation had been convulsing with pain, suffering and injustice for a long time.

The first sacrifice, after all, had been quickly followed by the first murder. The ground was splattered with Abel's blood by his brother Cain. From that bloodstained ground came The Cry for justice—for God set things right.[13]

Now imagine The Cry across the entire span of human history—all the acts of violence, injustice, and suffering—all the cries of all the innocent going up for centuries…

The God of the Bible always hears The Cry.

That's who he is—the good God of justice.

---

12 Heb 10:1-2 (see also Col 2:17).
13 Gen 4:10.

What was one of the central stories in the Old Testament?

That Yahweh heard the cries of those under the whips of Egypt.[14]
And he brings redemption and justice to Israel.

And what was one of the central promises of the Old Testament?

Yahweh will bring blessing through Abraham's family.[15]
He will bring redemption and justice to the world.

The terrible tension came, however, when Israel actually became Egypt.
Israel itself began making people cry out. And how could Yahweh
possibly bring blessing to the world when those who should have been
standing for justice were making the problem worse?

So Yahweh became an Israelite himself.
He became the true Israelite. The faithful Israelite.

The Israelite who would finally bring blessing to the world.

What would it mean to be true, to be faithful, to bring blessing?
It would mean sacrifice.

Mystery of mysteries—Yahweh himself went to the cross.

On the cross in Jesus, God became the final sacrifice that finally dealt
with all The Cry for justice throughout history. All those cries converged
on the cross until God himself actually cried out, *"My God, My God, why
have you forsaken me?"*[16]

---

14 Ex 2:23.
15 Gen 12:2, 18:18, 22:18
16 Matt 27:46, Mk 15:34.

God converged The Cry for justice and the crippling weight of the all the world's horrors at the cross. To all our surprise, Yahweh became flesh and allowed his blood to be spilled all over the rocky Judaean soil.

But somehow in his love, Jesus' blood *speaks a better word than the blood of Abel.*[17] The Cry of Abel's blood—and all the other cries throughout human history—could only speak a justice of condemnation. But the blood of Jesus cries out a justice of mercy.

God-Made-Flesh took all injustice, all violence, all darkness into and onto himself on the cross. God answered every cry for justice across the centuries through Jesus condemned and crucified.[18]

God sacrificed himself.

This moment was most clearly anticipated in ancient Israel's **Day of Atonement.** This was the one moment during Israel's year when all their sin was dealt with.[19] *On this day atonement will be made for you, to cleanse you. Then, before the LORD, you will be clean from all your sins.*[20] On this day, Yahweh purged Israel of its guilt and impurity. On this day, a pair of goats took the punishment that should have fallen on the community—death and exile.[21]

The holy God and his corrupt people were reconciled.
The Giver-of-Life and the takers-of-life, brought together.

Atonement was realized.

---

17 Heb 12:24b.
18 Rom 3:21-26.
19 Lev 16 (specifically see verses 15-22 and 34).
20 Lev 16:30.
21 See Lev 16. One goat was slain while the other one was banished (that is, went into permanent exile).

But year after year the Day of Atonement came and went. Year after year, the high priest (the bridge between Yahweh and Israel) performed this ceremony for the people. He kept having to do it. And his successor did it too. And his too. Year after year. It's like the ceremony couldn't stick —like it anticipated something else.

Christians have understood the cross to be the one moment in human history when all of the sins, corruption, rebellion and violence of the entire world were dealt with once and for all.[22]

The cosmic Moment of Atonement
for all people everywhere.[23]

Jesus gave one sacrifice and now he's done.[24]

He offered himself as a sacrifice.

Both the Offering and the Offerer. The Gift and the Giver.
The Final Sacrifice given by the Supreme High Priest.[25]

By trusting the sacrifice of our high priest, we can draw near to God with confidence. Both when we suffer injustice under the hand of Egypt and when we become Egypt. All the death we experience in the world and all the death that we contribute to the world—all of it has been dealt with.

None of it will keep us separated from the God of life.[26]
God reconciled the cosmos back to himself in Jesus.[27]

---

22 Heb 9:1-15 (compare with Lev 16).
23 1 John 2:2.
24 Heb 10:11-13.
25 Heb 7:22-27.
26 Heb 10:19-22.
27 2 Cor 5:19.

But the beautiful kaleidoscope of the Bible does not simply give us one image for the death of Jesus. The Bible is smarter than us (let's just face facts), and it continually invites us into a deeper and richer understanding of reality. The Day of Atonement is just one image helping us recognize the centrality, finality and universality of Jesus' death. But at least one other image is also in view:

Passover.

It was not by chance that Jesus was executed during the week of Passover.[28] This was the week Israel celebrated liberation from Egypt. And this was a rescue that came in the midst of Yahweh bringing judgment on Egypt. Israel long-remembered how they were spared judgment from Yahweh by seeking refuge under the blood of a sacrificed lamb.[29]

By choosing to go to the cross during Passover, Jesus became closely associated with its lamb.[30] His blood is the blood that shelters us from the judgment and wrath of God.[31]

Is there a subject that makes our culture—and much of the church— more uncomfortable than God's judgment and wrath? We need to understand that God's judgment and wrath are not arbitrary. They are not excessive. God is not angry over quibbles or trifles. He's not the meter-maid of the universe dealing out fire and brimstone for trivialities.

God *must* destroy everything destroying the earth.[32]
Because he's a good God.

---

28 Matt 26:17-19, Mk 14:1-16, Lk 22:7-16, Jn 13:1.
29 Ex 12:1-30.
30 e.g. Isa 52:13-53:12, Jn 1:29, Acts 8:26-35, Rev 5:6-10.
31 1 Thess 1:10.
32 Rev 11:18b.

Would we want him to do any differently?

To let evil just go unchecked?

A god with no anger over injustice would be worse than us because we certainly feel anger when we see it. The corruption, arrogance and injustice infecting and splintering the world must be dealt with.

In the exodus, both Egypt and Pharaoh arrogantly hardened themselves against Yahweh. They chose oppression, violence and death. And they are not alone. All sorts of people, powers and systems harden themselves against the redemptive purposes of the good Creator.[33] And God must bring their stubborn, damnable rebellion to an end. Those who insist on destroying the earth must be destroyed. But God saves everyone humble enough to seek refuge under the blood of the Lamb.

There is tension here between the wideness and the narrowness of the cross—between the Day of Atonement and Passover.

And we must not flatten this tension.

Jesus' sacrifice is both.

The tension we feel here brings us back to the mystery of God's absolute power and real human choice. God's real desire is to bring all of creation —including every single human being—back into his arms. How could God have made it any clearer? What other religion, philosophy or worldview understands the Divine as having faced real suffering and death to bring restoration and life?

The psalmist once cried in despair, "*No one can redeem the life of another or give to God a ransom for them—the ransom for a life is costly,*

---

[33] Eph 6:12, This is the meaning of much of the symbology behind Rev 13, 17-19.

no payment is ever enough—so that they should live on forever and not see decay.'[34]

Just one life is too costly. But *what is impossible with man is possible with God.*[35] For Yahweh himself did exactly this in Jesus. He entered into his own creation and ransomed all of humanity.[36]

No one can redeem and ransom?
Jesus can and did.

But evidently people have the ability to spurn the gift of the Passover Lamb. Some freely, arrogantly, tragically reject God's real desire to save them. The Bible holds out sincere hope for all to choose life[37] while recognizing that some will continue in death.[38]

In his death, Jesus bore the curse we deserve[39]
to grant us healing and forgiveness.[40]

And this sacrifice is bigger than we have dared to dream, because the Bible talks about Jesus' sacrificial death in ways that go far beyond the "personal salvation" emphasized almost exclusively in many Western pulpits. This sacrifice was indeed for individuals (thank God for that!) but it is much much bigger than that.

---

34 Ps 49:7-9.

35 Lk 18:27. In its context, Jesus is proclaiming that God can indeed save those whom it seems incredibly unlikely, namely the rich. And he shows this as true in the next chapter with a wee little man named Zaccheus.

36 Matt 10:28, Mk 10:45, 1 Timothy 2:6a, 1 Jn 2:2.

37 Rom 5:18-19, 11:25-32; 1 Tim 2:1-4, 4:10; 2 Pet 3:9.

38 Matt 25:31-46, Jn 3:16-18, 2 Thess 1:8-10, Rev 14:9-12, 20:11-15.

39 Gal 3:10-14 talks about Jesus *becoming* a curse for us. This probably refers to the curses spelled out in Deuteronomy 28:15-68 that will result if Israel breaks the Sinai covenant. In his sacrificial death, Jesus mysteriously absorbed that curse—in addition to the curses over all creation in Gen 3:14-19—so that the new covenant of Deuteronomy 30:1-6 can be extended. For more, see N.T. Wright, *Climax of the Covenant* (Minneapolis: Fortress Press, 1993), 137-156.

40 Isa 53:5 and 1 Pet 2:24.

It's much better than that.

It's much more beautiful than that.

The death of Jesus is about creating one new humanity
and bringing peace between different groups of people.[41]

It's about publicly humiliating
the Pharaohs or Caesars of today
who wield the sword as power.[42]

It's about daring to proclaim
that God has reconciled everything
in the universe back himself.[43]

The final sacrifice is about more than just personal salvation,
but it's certainly not about less.

And so how are we—as communities and as individuals—
to respond to the sacrificial death of Jesus?

Ironically with sacrifices.

Mind you, these sacrifices have nothing to do with rescuing ourselves or
reconciling anything in the universe back to God. Rather, learning to live
sacrificially is the only sane response to the generosity of God's sacrifice.

What else can we do?

41 Eph 2:13-22.
42 Col 2:13-15.
43 2 Cor 5:18-19, Col 1:19-23.

Rescued from rebellion,
Christians are to devote their lives
to doing good and sharing with others.[44]

Brought into light, we are to care for
the powerless, the downtrodden, and the forgotten.[45]

Purified from corruption, we must offer all our lives—
corporately and individually—as a living sacrifice.[46]

Learning to live sacrificially is the only sane thing to do.

If we're not learning to live lives of sacrifice, we don't really believe the good news. Or we don't really don't understand or appreciate this final sacrifice. Or we're really not interested in the heart of Jesus beating in our chests. For his heart is sacrificial, and he'll have ours be the same.

Everything in the world has been taken care of.

Everything wrong has been dealt with.

The bill has been paid in full; all that's left is gratuity… to learn to live in thankfulness and wonder of the majestic beauty of our self-giving love of God. And once we realize we're rescued—once we realize that we're saved by the Passover Lamb—we're invited out of Egypt.

We're invited to join the True Exodus.

---

[44] Heb 13:15-16.
[45] Ja 1:27.
[46] Rom 12:1.

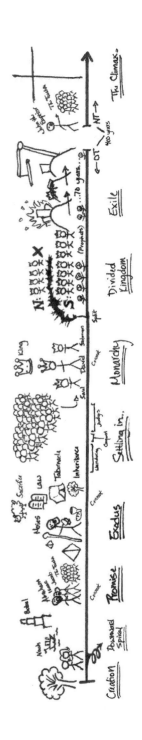

Creation | Backward Spiral | Promise | Exodus | Settling in. | Monarchy | Divided Kingdom | Exile | The Climax

15 the true exodus

The driving story of the Bible is of a God who sets slaves free. The Jewish people recounted the exodus century after century. How Yahweh had overthrown the oppressive power of Egypt; how he set them free from their bondage. Yahweh's desire was for his people to flourish and be free. The Creator is a Redeemer.

But as grand as the exodus was, there were simply some things that Yahweh's victory over Egypt didn't do. It didn't change the hearts of the Israelites. They rebelled against Yahweh—again and again—driving Moses to even offer himself in their place.[1] They couldn't obey Yahweh; they couldn't choose life.

It's like they were enslaved to something deeper.

By the first century, God's people saw Rome as the latest Egypt. And they were waiting for the Prophet-like-Moses who would liberate them politically, economically and socially. Their thoughts were, quite reasonably, focused on Roman oppression. They didn't anticipate that this Prophet-like-Moses would destroy the deepest bondage enslaving them (and all of humanity).

The slavery of sin, chaining us to death.

---

1 Ex 32:31-32.

But the earliest Christians proclaimed that the coming Prophet-like-Moses had finally arrived.[2] And this Prophet actually *did* die in place of the ungodly—even while they were still rebelling.[3]

Because Yahweh himself actually did what Moses proposed.
He did it in Jesus. And he did it on a cosmic scale.

The New Testament, after all, begins with deep resonances of Jesus as this new and greater Moses. In his account of Jesus' birth, Matthew recalls the twisted decrees of a tyrant to kill baby boys. Sound familiar?

But events have circled back around a terrifying irony:
This is happening in Bethlehem not Egypt.

This tyrant is not Pharaoh;
this tyrant is the king of the Jews.[4]

The Christmas story begins like an exodus story.

Another easy but significant nod to Moses can be glimpsed at Jesus' transfiguration. Remember Jesus ascending the mountain and becoming electric white? Who was he seen in the company of? That's right—Moses and Elijah.[5] And on intriguing note, Luke includes the subject of their conversation: the "*exodus*" that Jesus was about to fulfill in Jerusalem.[6]

Jesus was preparing to lead an exodus.

---

2 Acts 3:22-23 & 7:37 quoting Deut 18:15, 18-19. See also Jn 1:25 for their anticipation of this Prophet.
3 Rom 5:6-8. John also cleverly weaves this theme into his gospel with an ironic statement of theological truth coming from the lips of Caiphas, the corrupt high priest (Jn 11:50 & 18:14).
4 Compare Ex 1:15-16 with Matt 2:16.
5 Matt 17:1-13, Mk 9:2-13, Lk 9:28-36.
6 Lk 9:31.Unfortunately, very few translations capture the weight and significance of Luke's word choice. But the word literally is "exodus," from which the second book of the Bible famously gets its name. Kudos to the New Living Translation and Eugene Peterson's *The Message,* which boldly go there.

He anticipated something world-changing and history-defining. He anticipated conquering death; he anticipated the resurrection.

No belief system of the first century, Jewish or otherwise, was looking for the messiah's resurrection from the dead. After the Babylonian exile, belief in the resurrection of the dead had developed in the Jewish worldview, even though it was not unanimously affirmed.[7] But generally speaking, the Jewish people came to believe that the resurrection of the dead would happen at the end of history when Yahweh would finally judge the world, sorting out evil and injustices.[8]

An occasional freakish story might circulate about someone being raised from the dead—that is, about someone being temporarily resuscitated from the dead—but everyone always died again.[9]

And everyone expected them to… because only at the end of history would death finally die. Until then no one was absolutely free from death *right now*.

But then came Jesus' resurrection.

The resurrection of Jesus surprised everyone. His resurrection from the dead was mind-blowing—the resurrection they expected to be coming at the end of history had actually already invaded the universe. A real human being was already utterly free of death.

Over and over again in the book of Acts, we find the followers of Jesus proclaiming that Jesus had been resurrected from the dead.[10] Their

---

7 In Acts 23:6-10, notice the heated reaction that "the resurrection of the dead" gets when Paul mentions it during a trial in front of two different groups.
8 Dan 12:1-3.
9 e.g. Jn 12:17.
10 Acts 1:22; 2:24, 32; 3:15; 4:2, 33; 5:30; 10:40; 13:30-37; 17:18, 32.

proclamation was not simply that someone who had previously been dead was back. That would just be another freakish story.

They weren't proclaiming a mere resuscitation.
They were proclaiming THE Resurrection already come.

This Pharaoh was no match for this Prophet.
Death has died in Jesus.

The Resurrection is here!
New Creation is here![11]

This is hysterically good news because it means that Jesus had (and still has!) brought the future, coming resurrection into the present.[12] The end of history has somehow been brought into the middle of history. The age-to-come has leaked into the present.

And they insisted that Jesus didn't conquer death to enjoy his splendid deathlessness alone. He defeated the oppressive slave-master of death on behalf of all humanity. The writer of Hebrews explains that Jesus *shared in [our] humanity so that by his death he might break the power of him who holds the power of death—that is, the devil—and free those who all their lives were held in slavery by their fear of death.*[13]

Jesus tasted death for all people. For everyone.[14]

The new and greater Moses is leading a new and greater exodus.

---

11 2 Cor 5:17.
12 Jn 11:25-26.
13 Heb 2:14-15.
14 Heb 2:9b.(see also Rom 6:10, 2 Cor 5:14).

Having vanquished death, Jesus leads all who are willing out of death's slavery and into true Life. In the words of Paul, *For since death came through a man, the resurrection of the dead comes also through a man. For as in Adam all die, so in Christ all will be made alive.*[15] Jesus brings life and immortality to all humanity.[16]

No games. No hyperbole.
No exaggeration. No metaphor.

Literally—immortality and life.

This is the Christian hope.

And, in all honesty, it truly is humanity's only hope.[17]

We might note again here how the universal language used above ("all" and "everyone") proclaims how almost embarrassingly excessive was Jesus' defeat of death. Absolutely everyone everywhere has been included. God desires all to free from the slavery of the grave. But serious and sobering warnings throughout the Bible declare the real danger of willfully and continually rejecting his reign—of rejecting life.

Jesus gives, grants and extends immortality and life to all.

But only those desperate enough to trust him, humble enough to follow him, empty enough to embrace him—only they can receive this gift. Only they can join the true exodus.

Our choices really do matter.

---

[15] 1 Cor 15:21-22.
[16] 1 Tim 4:10b.
[17] Despite the advances of humanity throughout the centuries, Paul's assessment in 1 Cor 15:19 and 15:36 still hold true.

There is an amazing day coming when the judgment of Jesus will cleanse the world of rebellion, corruption and death. But this will inevitably and tragically include those who choose to stay in (or worse, promote) death.[18]

So what is the only sane response to the death of death?

What is the only sensible road to take
in the face of this Exodus?

The road out of Egypt, of course.

We're talking about **repentance**. We could use a different word if you'd like—a less churchy sounding word. But however we cut it, we're talking about changing the way we live, both actions and thinking.[19]

This is the only response that makes sense on any rational level. After all, if we really believe this jaw-dropping news of Jesus defeating death, we must change.[20] We've got to stop walking the old paths of rebellion, isolation, self-sufficiency and pride—the paths of death.

Pharaoh and Egypt have been conquered...
...so we've got to stop walking Egyptian roads.

Why would we stay?

But anyone who has tried to abandon these paths of death can tell you that it often feels almost impossible. It feels as if there's something so

---

18 Acts 17:31, 24:14-16, 2 Thess 1:5-10, Rev 20:11-15.
19 The Hebrew word for repent literally means "turn around" while the Greek word means to "change your mind."
20 e.g. Acts 2:32-39, 3:17-19.

absolutely dead inside of us that we cannot change ourselves. We seem to choose death every single time.

And it feels like this because it's true.

We cannot simply decide to change the deepest parts of ourselves in the same way that we casually decide to flip a light switch or what we'll have for lunch. It's too deep for that—we might as well be talking about changing our personality traits.

Humanity has become so chained to death by selfishness and sin that we find ourselves in chains that we cannot break. We cannot change— cannot repent—without God's work. Period.

But the good news is that Jesus has already defeated death and that his Spirit is already at work, making repentance, change and ultimately transformation possible.[21]

The all-powerful God gives you the free choice to repent.[22]

This is (again) the tension between God's power and man's choice. God will not force you or anyone else into repentance. He does not force anyone off the old paths of death—regardless of the fact that those roads are closed forever and they lead absolutely nowhere.

This tension is nicely summarized when Paul writes:

> Therefore, my dear friends, as you have always obeyed—not only in my presence, but now much more in my absence—continue to work out your salvation with fear and trembling, for it is God who works in you to will and to act in order to fulfill his good purpose.[23]

---

21 Rom 7:14-8:4 which serves as the fulfillment of passages like Jer 31:31-34 and Ezk 36:24-27.
22 The church father Augustine said, "So while [God] made you without you, he does not justify you without you." (Sermon 169).
23 Phil 2:12-13.

We work, repent and obey because God is already working. Because Jesus has already set us free. The two go hand-in-hand, as much as we might sometimes like to separate one or the other.

Those who freely choose to follow Jesus on this exodus out of death—to enter into Life—are always dependent on God's Spirit. Dependent on what he has already done in the world and what he still does in those who are willing.

This is the consistent drum-beat that Paul writes to his churches. Because of the sacrifice of King Jesus which defeated death—and because his Spirit continues to work—we are to respond with repentance.[24]

Sensible change. Sane change.
Grateful change. Joyful change.

Christians repent because we've heard a heartbeat in the otherwise chaotic corpse of human history.

In one of his letters, Paul spends a great deal of time talking about the implications of Jesus' resurrection, insisting—among other things—that our resurrection is coming too. Then he sums up his sweeping thoughts with a chilling, poetic mockery of death.[25]

But what follows that?

How would you follow up singing about death's execution?

---

[24] e.g. Rom 12:1-2, 2 Cor 7:1, Gal 4:1-7, Eph 4:1, Col 3:1-4, Phil 1:27. These are the hinges showing our action as response to what Jesus has accomplished. Always in that order.
[25] The chapter is 1 Cor 15, with v55-57 being the celebration of death's end.

Paul does it this way: *Stand firm. Let nothing move you. Always give yourselves fully to the work of the Lord, because you know that your labor in the Lord is not in vain.*[26]

The defeat of death compels us to truly live.

Life matters because death has died.
Life matters because the Resurrection is coming.

Life matters enough
to stop walking
the paths of death.

Because the Resurrection has already invaded earth.

And he has a name.
And he gives nail-scarred hugs.

The True Exodus is a liberation out of slavery and into slavery, if you want to think of that way. It's been said that we're all slaves to something —and Jesus gives us the change to be enslaved to joy, enslaved to grace, enslaved to hope.

Enslaved to Life.
It may seem impossible to shake off our old, familiar patterns of death. But we're invited to trust again and again in the reality of Jesus' resurrection and the work of God's Spirit in us. His Spirit makes it possible for us to become obedient in our deepest parts—to become alive in our deepest parts. We are redeemed from being the ever-dying slaves of rebellion so that we can be ever-living slaves of God. [27]

---

26 1 Cor 15:58.
27 Rom 6:15-23.

This is the life-long exodus of the Christian life: to keep in step with the Spirit of Jesus and discover that we're entering true life. And to trust with more and more confidence that Resurrection will come for us too.

Jesus leads a motley-crew of ragamuffins out of Egypt. We've done nothing to earn a ticket. Done nothing to participate in this exodus from death. All we can do is begin to believe it.

Because Yahweh has established the long-awaited new covenant, and it's entirely a gift. We simply trust him. Not merely for our sake but for the sake of the world. And that's another way of saying:

by grace,
through faith,
for good works.

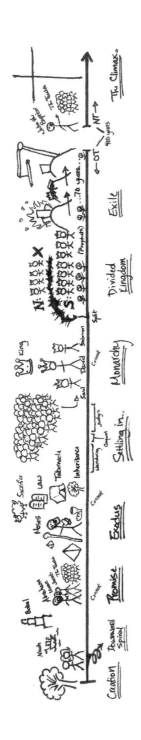

16 the new covenant

The Bible began with the all-powerful Creator creating a good world and endowing its inhabitants with freedom. Freedom to live in harmony with him. But his creation used its freedom to rebel and fell under a curse. So this Creator resolved that he would bless this creation again. Through a nation. Through Israel.[1]

God is faithful and would not abandon his creation.

But what happens when the cure becomes part of the cancer?
What happens when the doctors become part of the disease?

Because that's exactly what happened.

Israel—charged with blessing the cursed creation—became cursed itself. The holy nation rebelled against the covenant forged on the peaks of Sinai. But Yahweh promised that he would renew, restore and forgive the rebels that bear his name.

God is faithful and would not abandon Israel. He would forge a new covenant with his people. The cancer would be cured.

Imagine the weight and significance, then, after the crucifixion of Jesus when a group of Jews branded as "Christians"[2] began claiming that

---

1 Genesis 12:2, 18:18, 22:18
2 Acts 11:26.

230

Yahweh's new covenant had now been established through the faithfulness of Jesus.

What Israel has been longing for.
What the world has been longing for.

A new covenant of blessing with Israel for all creation.

As a refresher, the word "covenant" shows up frequently through the Old Testament, and isn't necessarily a religious word. It simply refers to a binding deal or legal agreement. Covenants were as common for Israel as contracts are for us.[3]

But one of the Old Testament's staggering claims is that the true God makes covenants with people. Specifically with Israel.

Sometimes those deals were one-sided. God alone commits himself to do something—like his covenants with both Abraham and David. He promises to bless Abraham (and the world) and a never-ending dynasty to David (the everlasting kingdom).[4]

These are covenants
that Yahweh promised
without qualification.

He would make good on them regardless of anything else.

But sometimes those deals were two-sided, with God making covenants that required the free participation of people. The most significant example of this was the covenant forged at Sinai between Yahweh and

---

[3] The word is versatile and can be used many different ways including as an agreement between people (1 Sam 20:16, 23:18) or even a commitment to oneself (Job 31:1).
[4] Abraham (Gen 12, 15, 17); David (2 Sam 7).

his recently-rescued Israelites. That covenant was *not* one-sided. Israel had responsibilities to fulfill. They were required to be a kingdom of priests.

Yahweh's nation of light bringing blessing to a darkened world.[5]

This was a deal requiring participation on two ends:

The people were to obey, choose life, and be a blessing.

IF they did this,
THEN God would
keep them in the land.[6]

Had they kept their side, Israel could have stayed in the land that was promised to Abraham. Most of Israel's story, however, recounts how they continually abandoned the Sinai covenant. Even though Yahweh continually rescued them—offering mercy, grace and second chances for centuries—they continued in rebellion. They continually rejected Yahweh's reign over them. Continually rejected the task they were elected for:

To be holy as God is holy.
To be like the good Creator.
To be his nation of blessing in the world.

And so Israel fell under the dreadful curse of exile.[7]

Under the command of leaders like Joshua, Yahweh used the Israelites as a scalpel of judgment—cutting out cancer in the land of promise. But

---

5 Ex 19:5-6.
6 Lev 18:24-28; Deut 8:22-28, 30:11-20
7 Deut 28:15-68 (specifically v15, 64-68).

then centuries later, Yahweh used empires like Assyria and Babylon to bring judgment on his own people because they themselves had now become the cancer. Israel wanted so badly to be like all the other nations that Yahweh finally scattered them among them.[8]

But what would this mean for Yahweh's promises? Israel definitely shattered the two-sided covenant of Sinai. But could they have somehow canceled his one-sided covenants?

These questions haunted Israel for centuries.

The prophets proclaimed the faithfulness of Yahweh—that he would eventually establish a new covenant. Moses had predicted it first.[9] But later prophets continued to proclaim this hope to Israel, with Jeremiah's words being some of the best remembered:

> *"The days are coming," declares the LORD, "when I will make a new covenant with the people of Israel and with the people of Judah. It will not be like the covenant I made with their ancestors when I took them by the hand to lead them out of Egypt, because they broke my covenant, though I was a husband to them," declares the LORD. "This is the covenant I will make with the people of Israel after that time," declares the LORD. "I will put my law in their minds and write it on their hearts. I will be their God, and they will be my people."*[10]

These words must have been like a shot of adrenaline. After all, the people of Judah had just been carted off to Babylon.

What incredible words of hope during the midst of their exile! What amazing comfort in the midst of their curse!

Their relentless unfaithfulness to the first covenant got them into this mess, but Yahweh would not abandon them forever.

---

8 e.g. Jer 5:19.
9 Deut 30:1-10.
10 Jer 31:31-34.

Because God is not unfaithful.

Ezekiel was another prophet proclaiming the hope of a new covenant. He conceded that Israel would have to face the consequences of their actions, but he assured them that Yahweh would eventually atone for their sins.[11]

The Israelites would not be under the curse of exile forever.

And so as the survivors of Judah eventually returned to the land and began rebuilding Jerusalem, they clung to these promises:

God is faithful.
A new covenant is coming.

But what will it look like? And how will he do it?

So it's extraordinary, shocking and beautiful when Jesus begins talking at his last Passover feast. He's talking about this long-awaited new covenant:

> While they were eating, Jesus took bread, and when he had given thanks, he broke it and gave it to his disciples, saying, "Take it; this is my body." Then he took a cup, and when he had given thanks, he gave it to them, and they all drank from it. "This is my blood of the covenant, which is poured out for many," he said to them. "Truly I tell you, I will not drink again from the fruit of the vine until that day when I drink it new in the kingdom of God."[12]

Yahweh promised he wasn't done with Abraham's family. That he would establish a new covenant with them to bless the world. And it's finally happening.

---

11 Ezk 16:59-63.
12 Mk 14:22-25 See also Matt 26:26-29, Lk 22:19-20, and 1 Cor 11:23-26.

And Jesus claims that the new covenant is being made *in him*... most mysteriously, through his broken body. In his crucifixion.

Yahweh forged a covenant that was eventually broken by the *faithlessness* of the Israelites. But now a new covenant has been forged by the *faithfulness* of one Israelite.

Yahweh became an Israelite to hold up both ends of the bargain. Sinai shattered? Very well, Yahweh descends to Calvary. He's now Covenant-Maker and Covenant-Keeper.

Here we find what Israel has been longing for, but it looks so very different than they imagined. Here we finally have a new covenant that brings blessing, forgiveness, renewal, and resurrection (in short, salvation) to the entire world. And this covenant is centered around the faithfulness of Jesus.

Jesus, the faithful God and the faithful Man.

But what exactly does this new covenant look like?

Who is included?
And what does it mean to participate?

Well, some of the earliest disciples began to realize that this new covenant includes more than just the Jewish people. This was particularly difficult for many of the early Christians (all of whom were Jewish) to wrap their minds around. But in the deepest ways, the faithfulness of Jesus meant that Israel's national task—to bless the world —has finally been accomplished. Israel's God finally made good on blessing the world through Abraham's family. And he did it by becoming part of the family himself. Now at last, divine blessing is flowing from Israel to all the nations.

The separation of Jew from Gentile isn't needed anymore.

The task is fulfilled,
the blessing is flowing,
all are welcome.

This is a new covenant extending to all people everywhere.

Throughout his letters, Paul insists that our inclusion in this new covenant is entirely God's work—we're absolutely powerless to "get in" or "secure it" at all:

Being born into the right group won't do it.
Neither will trying to get into the right group.

We can't say the right thing or pray the right prayer.
And good "religious" activities won't help either.[13]

As Eugene Peterson writes, "We become Christians because we realize we cannot save ourselves and need Christ to save us."[14]

Which is another way of saying: *For it is by grace you have been saved, through faith—and this is not from yourselves, it is the gift of God—not by works, so that no one can boast.*[15]

---

[13] In fact, trying to secure membership in the people-of-God in these ways is evidence that one does not understand the free gift of the membership being offered (Gal 5:1-6).
[14] Eugene Peterson, *The Wisdom of Each Other* (Grand Rapids: Zondervan, 1998), 32.
[15] Eph 2:8-9.

Inclusion in the new covenant (that is, participation in the forgiveness, blessing, renewal and resurrection of all things) comes freely to everyone who trusts the life-giving, covenant-making God revealed in Jesus.

To everyone who denounces
the serpent's lie to be "gods."

To everyone who abandons
rebellious, damnable self-sufficiency.

To everyone willing to admit
that they're utterly, hopelessly dead.

And to everyone who trusts
the God of the cross for new life.

We enter into the blessing of the new covenant by **grace** alone.

We can only ever **believe** this grace.
We can only **trust** that God really has included us too.

Because he already has.

Those who trust this God are "righteous" or "right with God."
Those who trust are part of the New Covenant People.[16]

The true "children of Abraham" are those who have faith like Abraham.[17] Who trust God. We are all scoundrels (like Abraham) who must take God at his word that he's including us. It doesn't matter if you're a Jew or a

---

16 For more on "righteousness" as covenant membership, I recommend sitting down with *What Saint Paul Really Said* by N.T. Wright, *The Future of Justification* by John Piper, and *Justification* by N.T. Wright—in that order. The third is a response to the second which is a response to the first.
17 Gal 3:7. See also Rom 4:3-5.

non-Jew—you are freely included in this new covenant.[18] When you recognize and trust in the faithfulness of Jesus, you realize that you've already been included in this new covenant.

The world has finally been blessed through Abraham's family.

Through King Jesus.[19]

And when we really trust this, we cannot help but be changed. Belief in the absurdly-free, life-giving, world-renewing blessing of the faithful and living God—well, that sort of thing changes you.

Inclusion in the new covenant means participating with this God.

The new covenant, after all, should never be confused with a country club where dues are paid and privileges are received. That's not far from the way Israel began to think about the first covenant: "This thing is all about us." This was never God's intent in electing Abraham or Israel, and it's still not his intent.

Participating in the new covenant means blessing the world.

> For it is by grace you have been saved, through faith—and this is not from yourselves, it is the gift of God—not by works, so that no one can boast. For we are God's handiwork, created in Christ Jesus to do good works, which God prepared in advance for us to do.[20]

Paul immediately follows *the how* we are included in God's saving covenant with *the why* we are included. They are inseparable.

By grace... *through* faith... *for* **good works.**

---

18 Eph 2:11-22.
19 Gal 3:16.
20 Eph 2:10.

Being the New-Covenant-People means becoming the kingdom-of-God-people. We are learning to trust our lives to King Jesus and to extend his life-giving reign into the world.

So the new covenant is *available to* all the world. But the new covenant also *works for* all the world. This is precisely what the prophet Isaiah envisioned when he declared a coming end to exile and blessing on God's people:

> *"It is too small a thing for you to be my servant to restore the tribes of Jacob and bring back those of Israel I have kept. I will also make you a light for the Gentiles, that my salvation may reach to the ends of the earth." ...This is what the LORD says:*
>
> ***"In the time of my favor I will answer you, and in the day of salvation I will help you; I will keep you and will make you to be a covenant for the people,*** *to restore the land and to reassign its desolate inheritances, to say to the captives, 'Come out,' and to those in darkness, 'Be free!'"*[21]

Isaiah glimpsed a day coming when Yahweh would establish a new covenant that would bring blessing to the world. God's rule and reign would be embodied in the world by God's people.

The New-Covenant-People have been elected—drafted even. Drafted into embodying God's salvation to everyone else.

Blessed to be a blessing;
elected for all the earth.[22]

---

[21] Isa 49:6, 8-9.

[22] I agree with scholars who understand the word "preordained/predestined" (particularly in Rom 8:29-30 and Eph 1:5, 11) along with the word "chosen/called/elected" (again, Rom 8:30 & other passages) as being primarily vocational. This general idea explored in Rom 9—11, regards Israel's vocation through history and whether God remains faithful to them. Paul wrestles painfully (9:1-5) with whether God's work through Israel has failed (9:6). Has Israel been cast aside (9:7-29) now that the Gentiles are being received as God's people (9:30, 11:11)? Has Jacob become Esau? Has Israel become Pharaoh? But God's irrevocable (11:29) *"purpose in election"* (9:11) has always been *"that [his] name might be proclaimed in all the earth"* (9:17) so that he can have mercy on all (10:4-12, 11:30-32). The elect were (and are) always chosen with the aim of saving more than the elect. The transformation of Rom 8:29-30 ought to be understood as another way of articulating the transformation of 2 Cor 3:18, 5:17-20. Those chosen are being transformed into the image of Christ for the sake of others.

A New-Covenant-People for the sake of the whole world.

Paul wanted the earliest Christians to catch this. In a letter to a church in a city called Corinth, he touches on this, insisting that they—the seriously mixed up group that they are!—have become the agents of this new covenant on behalf of the world:[23]

> God made him who had no sin to be sin for us, so that in him we might become the righteousness of God. As God's co-workers we urge you not to receive God's grace in vain. For he says, **"In the time of my favor I heard you, and in the day of salvation I helped you."** I tell you, now is the time of God's favor, now is the day of salvation.[24]

Paul actually quotes Isaiah's prophecy about the new covenant. Isaiah had talked about a time when God's people would *"be a covenant"* for all the earth. Well, now it's here. It's now. It's today.

We live in the long-awaited day of Yahweh's salvation, and Christians have been drafted as its agents.

This makes absolute sense because in his first sermon, Jesus himself described his mission this way: *to proclaim good news to the poor. He has sent me to proclaim freedom for the prisoners and recovery of sight for the blind, to set the oppressed free, to proclaim the year of the Lord's favor.*[25]

Jesus brought the rule and reign of God into existence around him through his actions. It only makes sense that those participating in his new covenant will embody what he has established.

Of course! What else could they do?

---

[23] 2 Cor 3:6a.
[24] 2 Cor 5:21-6:2.
[25] Lk 4:18b-19.

The Church—as a gathering of the drafted—has responsibility. We are called to allow the uprightness and justice of God to be transforming every aspect of our lives. And then we are to enact and embody this uprightness and justice for the sake of others.

By grace.
Through faith.
For good works.

God's people for the sake of all the world… that's what the New-Covenant-People are all about.

So to be a Christian is to be intimately acquainted with invitation.

We ourselves have embraced God's invitation to participate in his redemption of the entire universe. This is all gift—all grace.

We are invited to trust that our faithlessness has not canceled God's faithfulness.[26] The invitation is to abandon guilt, despair, and all other self-preoccupation and to lose ourselves in the beautiful gaze of the faithful God-man who reclaims the lost.[27] The invitation is to trust that we are forgiven.[28] All we can do is trust that it's already done—already true.

And then (quite naturally) we are invited to participate in spreading the goodness of this God into the people and world around us.

We're invited to invite others.

Because absolutely everyone everywhere is invited.

---

[26] Rom 3:3.
[27] See Jesus' parables in Luke 15 for the shocking and stubborn forgiveness of God.
[28] Eph 4:32; Col 2:13, 3:13; 1 Jn 2:12.

The drafted declare grace to all.

The drafted invite all to trust—all to have faith.

The drafted embody good works in the world.

This is what it looks like when the self-sacrificing heart of the Father, Son, and Spirit moves into town.

This is what it looks like when God is with us.

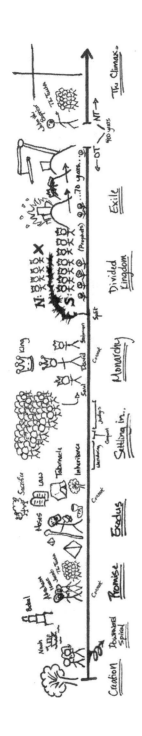

17 god with us

The Bible's long story declares how God refuses to abandon his creation. As creation spiraled downward into rebellion, the Creator promised to bless the world through Abraham's family. Eventually he himself entered that rebellious family as his promised blessing. He himself became the King whose healing reign would go on forever. He himself forged a new covenant through the blood of his own sacrificial death. And his very resurrection establishes a new exodus into true and everlasting life.

Jesus is the climax of Israel's story and human history.
The Creator never abandoned his creation.

The earliest Christians began to understand that Jesus—that dusty rabbi who ate meals and drank wine with them—actually created the universe.

They had actually met the Creator himself.[1]

Now it's quite possible to learn much about this Creator by looking around at his creation.[2] The beauty of the changing seasons, the marvel that is the expanding universe, the intricate complexity of DNA, the infectious laugh of a child—from these things we can glimpse something of God's creativity, God's power, God's intelligence and God's joy.

Looking at creation can tell us *about* God.

---

1 See Jn 1:1-3, Acts 3:15, Col 1:15-20, Heb 1:1-3.
2 Rom 1:19-20.

But looking at creation cannot *introduce* God.

Observation and reflection cannot tell us God's name, as it were.

But the earliest Christians proclaimed that God himself has, in fact, introduced himself. And he has done it in two parts:

Part one, he introduced himself at the burning bush to Moses.[3] His name is Yahweh, and he alone is the true God. He is loving, good and just.[4] Although Israel might be tempted to worship other so-called-gods, they're nothing but lies and lifeless idols.

Hi, my name is Yahweh—I am what "the Divine" is like.

Part two, he introduced himself as the man named Jesus. Yahweh made himself known to us in an absolutely head-spinning way. Face-to-face.[5] Through his actions, his teachings and his very presence, Jesus made it clear that God is involved far more intimately with humanity than any of us ever dared to dream.

Hi, my name is Jesus—I am what Yahweh is like.

God introducing himself as the man named Jesus takes us deeper into the mysterious heart of the universe than Moses, Israel or we ever expected. It allows us—indeed, it compels us—to reflect on the beauty of both "the incarnation" and "the Trinity."[6]

---

3 Ex 3:14-15.
4 See Ex 34:5-7.
5 e.g. Jn 1:18.
6 Neither of these words is found in the Bible. Rather they are terms the church has used to talk about what we do find in the Bible, namely God becoming man in Jesus and the pattern of God revealed as Father, Son and Spirit.

There's a lot of chit-chat about "God" in the world. To talk about "God" can mean a lot of things. But until we engage these two realities, we're not really talking about the God revealed in Jesus. With these two revelations, we can begin speaking—stuttering and stammering, really—about the true, mysterious and living God.

So first—to the **incarnation**.
The Divine-made-human.

All four gospels make amazing assertions about Jesus' connection with Israel's God. Matthew, for example, opens his rendition of the story by recapping the entire Old Testament in 17 verses.[7] Only then does he plunge straight into what his gospel is going to be about—how Yahweh will save Israel (and the entire world for whom they exist) from their sins. He will do it through a child about to be born.[8]

This child will show that he has not abandoned Israel or the world.

For his child is called Immanuel.
This child is "God with us."[9]

That theme continues right through to the end of Matthew's gospel when Jesus assures his disciples that he will always be Immanuel—even to the end of the age.[10] Could Matthew be any clearer?

When you're with Jesus, you're with God.

---

[7] Matt 1:1-17. By contrast, it took me ten chapters—Matthew's just showing off.
[8] Matt 1:21 (compare especially with Psalm 130).
[9] Matt 1:23.
[10] Matt 28:20. See Matt 18:20 as another example of the theme popping up its head.

John, as another example, begins his gospel with a great echo of the Bible's opening song.[11] God—along with his ever-present Word and Spirit—had always been there at the beginning. And now that God has *made his dwelling among us.*[12]

When John says the Divine has "made his dwelling among us," he's actually turning the word "tabernacle" into a verb. God is "tabernacling" with us. Yahweh—whose glorious presence filled the universe at its beginnings and a tent/temple during Israel's history—has done the impossible. He has become human himself.

Pillars of cloud and fire, now flesh and blood.

In subtle and also straightforward ways, the gospel writers describe the impossible—what the church throughout history has traditionally termed "the Incarnation." The world's Creator—Yahweh, the God of Israel—made himself intimately knowable.

It's hard to wrap our minds around the implications of this staggering claim. We've become calloused to it. One New Testament scholar pushes us to reflect further on it:

> Now: let us suppose that *this* God were to become human. What would such a God look like? This is the really scary thing that [many people] never come to grips with; not that Jesus might be identified with a remote, lofty, imaginary being (any fool could see the flaw in that idea), but that God, the real God, the one true God, might actually look like Jesus. And not a droopy, pre-Raphaelite Jesus, either, but a shrewd Palestinian Jewish villager, who drank wine with his friends, agonized over the plight of his people, taught in strange stories and pungent aphorisms, and was executed by the occupying forces.[13]

---

11 Gen 1:1 and Jn 1:1.
12 Jn 1:14 (for examples of "the Word of God" see Gen 1:3, Isa 40:6-8, Isa 55:10-11).
13 N.T. Wright, *Who Was Jesus?* (Grand Rapids: Eerdmans, 1992), 52.

The real God, the one true God, might actually look like Jesus.
In the moments we begin believing this, our heads spin and our knees tremble and our hearts melt. The infinite and unfathomable Mystery behind all reality became finite and knowable. In Jesus, the Deity now has a seeable, touchable, kissable face.[14]

So this Mystery has also shown his cards.
It is not beneath the Deity to become a human.

He is a God willing to walk with us, eat with us, laugh with us, cry with us, suffer alongside us and taste death for us.

Think on that: God knows precisely what it's like to be human—in every way. He knows what it's like. Every bit of it. He has become like us in every respect. Minus our rebellion and corruption.[15]

The story of Jesus is the story of God *with us.*
The story of God *for us.*

Of course, the Israelites had long celebrated a physical reminder of God's presence. For centuries the sight of the tabernacle (and later the temple) reassured the Israelites that Yahweh was with them. But as Jesus walks the dusty streets of Palestine in the Gospels, he completely overshadows the temple.

That temple rebuilt by Ezra, Nehemiah and Zerubbabel that aimed to recapture some of the glory of Solomon's world-wonder—it's now being overshadowed by the glory of the World-Maker.

---

14 1 Jn 1:1.
15 Heb 4:15.

The gospel writers assume that Jesus is a living, breathing Temple. In both his words[16] and his actions,[17] Jesus is the ultimate place where people encounter Yahweh.

Jesus goes so far as to condemn the temple in Jerusalem. He proclaims judgment and coming doom on both it and its corrupt religious leaders. And in case anyone was fuzzy on what he was saying would happen to the temple, he withers a fig tree.[18]

Later that week, when he's hanging on the cross, accusers taunt Jesus, *"So! You who are going to destroy the temple and build it in three days, come down from the cross and save yourself!"*[19] But they misunderstood him. He would indeed rebuild a ruined temple.

The Temple being crucified.[20]

For centuries Yahweh had given earth a taste of his presence. He had dwelt with Israel. At Sinai and Zion. In the tabernacle and the temple. But now something greater than the temple has arrived.[21]

Jesus of Nazareth is the living, breathing, walking, talking Temple. The truest place where heaven and earth meet.
The place where God and mankind come together.

But then after his resurrection, Jesus ascended into heaven.

---

16 e.g. In Matt 12:1-6, Jesus compares the devotion of priests to Yahweh in the temple to his disciples devotion to him.
17 e.g. Mk 2:7 (Matt 9:6 & Lk 5:24), which shows Jesus offering the forgiveness for sins that could only have been granted through the sacrificial system at the temple. Jesus is himself acting as the temple.
18 Matt 21:12-22, Mk 11:12-21. The temple itself will wither in 70 AD, when Rome burns it to the ground.
19 Mk 15:29b-30 (Matt 27:40). See also testimony in the trials (Matt 26:60b, Mk 14:57) and Jesus' actual words in the temple cleansing in John (Jn 2:19).
20 Jn 2:21.
21 Matt 12:6.

This is a bit perplexing. Why did he do this? It's not exactly the way most of us would have done it. We would prefer a Jesus that we could still see and touch. Jesus insists, however, that it's actually good that he's leaving.[22]

This shows the radical difference between the true God and us. We're the impatient control-freaks. He is not.

He is the tireless, patient God
who redeems from the inside.

He reconciled creation and reoriented history through Jesus.
From the inside.

And now he redeems and transforms us in the same way.
From the inside.

Jesus can honestly say it's better that he's going away. God dwelling intimately *among* his people was just an appetizer—now the main course is arriving! Get ready, Jesus says, because Yahweh is planning to dwell intimately *within* his people.[23] And he has made good on this promise.

Fifty days after Passover—on the anniversary of Yahweh descending in fire on Sinai—God's Spirit descends in fire on the disciples.[24] At the first Pentecost, Yahweh descended to give instruction. This time Yahweh descends to give himself. His Spirit invades those desperate and humble enough to trust him.

---

22 Jn 16:7.
23 Acts 1:1-8.
24 Acts 2:1-4. The word "Pentecost" is the Greek translation for "fifty."

And this is one of the early scandals of the Christian message. That God does not live in the temple of Jerusalem[25] or any Greek temple.[26] Yahweh does not dwell on a mountain—not Sinai, Zion or anywhere else.

Absolutely revolutionary.

No wonder Christians were decried and denounced as heretics by the Jews and atheists by Romans. But what else could they do? They had to proclaim the truth—the Spirit of God dwells in the people who submit themselves to the reign of Jesus.[27]

The people of Jesus are the place that the Divine dwells.
The people of Jesus are the temple of the living God.

The revolution of God's invading Spirit brings us to the church's celebration of God as three-in-one. Christians have historically affirmed **the Trinity**—that God is a "triune" God. This emerges from the pattern of Yahweh revealing himself in Scripture as Father, Son and Holy Spirit. While shadows of this can be seen as early as Genesis, the pattern becomes explicit in the New Testament.[28]

The question of what God is like—better, of who God is—lies at the center of the Christian faith. The "who" for Christians is Father, Son and Spirit. This understanding of God flows directly out of our understanding of Jesus as God-with-us:

---

[25] Acts 7:44-50.
[26] Acts 17:22-25.
[27] 1 Cor 3:16; 2 Cor 6:16; Eph 2:19-22, 5:15-20 talk about the community being filled with the Spirit, while 1 Cor 6:18-20 talks about individual Christians being temples of the Spirit.
[28] e.g. In Genesis 1:1-3 we find God, his Spirit, and his spoken Word, God speaks in the plural in 1:26. Yahweh appearing to Abraham as three strangers in Gen 18.

Jesus is (true) God in the flesh, but then we find him—this (true) human —praying to Yahweh as his Father.[29] And furthermore (as we've already seen) Jesus talks about the Spirit of God which will indwell his followers after he leaves.[30] All three are assumed to be truly God, yet somehow they're distinct.

Jesus is God *with* us. The Spirit is God *within* us.
The one[31] true God is revealed in the three.[32]

Three in one? Who would ever have imagined such a thing?

Precisely. Intimately immanent yet mysteriously transcendent. The God who is familiar and touchable in Jesus is also beyond all comprehension and expectation.

Father, Son and Spirit.
The One God.

The Trinity is not a mere detachable extra to the Christian faith. How we understand God shapes the way we understand life. So in his masterful *Mere Christianity*, C.S. Lewis explains some of the daily and practical implications of understanding God as Trinity:

> An ordinary simple Christian kneels down to say his prayers. He is trying to get into touch with God. But if he is a Christian he knows that what is prompting him to pray is also God: God, so to speak, inside him. But he also knows that all his real knowledge of God comes through Christ, the Man who was God-—that Christ is standing right beside him, helping him to pray, praying

---

29 e.g Matt 14:23, Mk 6:46, Lk 6:12
30 e.g. Jn 15:26, 16:12-15.
31 The oneness of God (monotheism) is foundational to both Judaism and Christianity. The foundational confession of Judaism in Deut 6:4 is reaffirmed by both Jesus (Mk 12:32) and the apostle Paul (Gal 3:20). But in light of Jesus, this confession about the one God now includes Jesus (1 Cor 8:6).
32 e.g. Matt 28:19, Acts 2:32-33, 2 Cor 13:14, Gal 4:6, Eph 1:17, Phil 3:3-4 Col 1:9-10, 1 Thess 1:2-4, 1 Pet 1:2-12.

for him. You see what is happening. God is the thing to which he is praying—the goal he is trying to reach. God is also the thing inside him which is pushing him on—the motive power. God is also the road or bridge along which he is being pushed to that goal. So that the whole threefold life of the three-personal Being is actually going on in that ordinary little bedroom where an ordinary man is saying his prayers.[33]

The Trinity matters for ordinary Christians living ordinary lives because the way we think about God shapes the way we think about life. And God as Father, Son and Spirit reassures us that we're not alone.

God's always desired to dwell intimately with humanity. This was his intent from the very beginning, to walk in the garden with his beloved dirt-people. At long last, in Jesus, God stuck his toes in the dirt and walked creation as a living, breathing temple. And now he's invading all those willing to receive his Spirit—they are becoming his home.[34]

And Christians anticipate a coming day when heaven and earth will finally be married. When we can finally see God dwelling with us. Finally walking among us.

And on that Day, there will be (thank God) no more temple.[35]

All of reality overrun and invaded by God himself.
All of reality will be the temple.[36]

---

[33] C.S. Lewis, *Mere Christianity* (New York: Harper Collins, 2001) 163. Lewis also gives another description that I find incredibly helpful:: "In God's dimension, so to speak, you find a being who is three Persons while remaining one Being, just as a cube is six squares while remaining one cube. Of course we cannot fully conceive a Being like that: just as, if we were so made that we perceived only two dimensions in space we could never properly imagine a cube" (162). In case you haven't realized from the number of quotes, you really should make reading *Mere Christianity* a priority.
[34] Rom 8:14-17 (and I might add 10:4-13) as well as Gal 4:4-7.
[35] Rev 21:22 (Evidently the intricate detail of the temple as envisioned in Ezk 40-48 is best read as metaphor.)
[36] Rev 21:3.

That's what's coming—heaven. It's coming and it's unstoppable. So as colonists of heaven, we prayerfully seek glimpses of that Day spilling into this day. To see the Spirit invade our lives and our world. And we can recognize plenty of signs that God's Spirit is already dwelling within us and among us.

Perhaps the only right place to start is the Church—the New Covenant People loving and caring for each other. The colonists of heaven actually united in love. It's extraordinarily difficult to die to our selfishness and be built into God's unified temple. But it's happening in more places and more often than despairing cynics or sensationalistic fault-finders choose to believe. We know that we're not alone when we see incredibly diverse people embracing their ultimate unity in Jesus.[37]

The Spirit is uniting us in love for each other.

We know that God is with us.

These people—united in Jesus—follow their King's example and embody the kingdom of God around them. They bring goodness, justice and light especially to areas of unpopularity, hostility and darkness. We know that we're not alone when the Church is actually behaving like the place where heaven and earth meet.[38]

The Spirit is breathing heaven into us and through us.

We know that God is with us.

And everyone everywhere can recognize that the marriage of heaven and earth hasn't fully arrived yet. And so the Spirit of God groans through

---

37 Eph 4:1-16.
38 1 Pet 4:12-17 (see 2:11-17 and 3:13-17 for examples of enacting the kingdom).

the Church for that day. The people of God recognize how the thorns and thistles of the curse still choke parts of creation. So we enter into the places of the world's great suffering, proclaiming that it won't always be this way. We hurt as we hope. We know that we're not alone when we prayerfully ache for the world.[39] The Spirit is groaning with labor pains in us.

We know that God is with us. The true and living God has made himself known. Yahweh has come and tabernacled among us.

We're not alone because God knows exactly what it's like. Jesus himself is the true Temple, destroyed and rebuilt. His Spirit invades all who will trust him, allowing us to approach God with confidence and participate in his rule and reign.[40]

The One God—Father, Son and Spirit—is *with* us.
And this God is *for* us.

We are becoming his dwelling place.

And now, we're beginning to sense humanity's true shape.

To understand the deepest meaning of our lives.
To understand why we follow God's instruction (God's "law").

We're beginning to understand what it means to be lovers.

---

[39] Rom 8:22-27.
[40] Heb 3:4, 10:19-25.

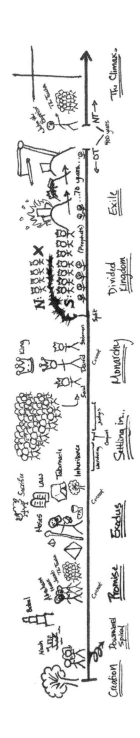

18 the law of love

Jesus reigns over the universe. And he is the King who graces his subjects with gifts. The people learning to submit to his reign are the same people who learn to receive these gifts.

Those honest enough to admit they are flatlining rebels.
Those desperate enough to confess they need his graces.
Those empty and open enough to be invaded by his Spirit.

It's all gift.
It's all grace.

But one of our King's foundational gifts has often been wildly misunderstood. His subjects have often maligned, marginalized and even reviled this gift.

We're talking, of course, about the King's instruction.
What is the place of law in the kingdom?

The law has been around for a while. Remember that after he delivered the Israelites from Egypt, Yahweh gave them his law at Mount Sinai. He gave them instruction for living—traditionally, the first five books of the Bible (the Torah).

They were no longer slaves. They had already been rescued or "saved." And so Yahweh intended these people—his kingdom of priests—to live in

258

a particular way. To be holy like him. In the wreckage after Eden and Babel, the Israelites were a people relearning what life was supposed to be like.

Living as Yahweh's people meant living by Yahweh's instruction. Yahweh's law was a magnificent gift, not a burden. Israel at its best understood this.[1]

Of course it's a gift.

A kingdom with no law would be chaos.

Life with no order would be death.

But after a millennium of instruction, Israel also gained plenty of experience rebelling against Yahweh's law. And so Yahweh banished them from the land with the judgment of exile. But after finally returning from their captivity in Babylon, Israel continued to trust that Yahweh had not abandoned them. Their God would fulfill his promises and finally establish his kingdom.

Anticipation and speculation mounted by the time of Jesus on how Yahweh would finally and decisively act. One particular group within Judaism, the Pharisees, believed that Yahweh would make his move— would finally establish his rule and reign—once the Jewish people finally learned to be faithful to the law.[2] The righteous should walk in obedient trust, remember?[3]

Emphasis on the obedient part.

---

[1] Notice how Torah is praised in Psalm 19 and the far lengthier Psalm 119.
[2] See passages such as Deut 30:9-10 and 2 Chr 7:14-18 for examples of the texts they emphasized.
[3] Hab 2:4.

And although the Pharisees typically get caricatured today as "bad guys" in many sermons, they were absolutely upstanding people. They worshipped and obeyed Yahweh, aching for the reign of Yahweh to fill the entire earth with justice and peace.[4]

But the Pharisees had also fallen into the trap of thinking that Yahweh favored Israel over and against the rest of the world. And if you didn't keep the law well enough (and they themselves got to determine what "well enough" meant) then even you—as a fellow Jew—might not really be a true "child of Abraham."

And they doubt you're really obeying like you should.

But from their worldview, it's easy to see why the Pharisees were critical of Jesus. He didn't seem to honor or obey Yahweh's law to the degree he should.

This backwoods prophet from Nazareth violated the Sabbath,[5] seemed to subvert the authority of Moses,[6] questioned the dietary laws,[7] and even challenged their very uprightness![8]

From their perspective, Jesus was leading the people away from obedience of Yahweh—was leading them towards disobedience.

The very definition of a false prophet.

Israel had strayed from Yahweh so many times throughout their history. The curse of exile had fallen on them, in large part, because the nation

---

4 Hab 2:14 (see also Isa 11:1-9).
5 e.g. Mk 3:1-6 (Matt 12:1-14, Lk 6:1-11).
6 e.g. Mk 10:1-12 (Matt 19:1-9).
7 Mk 7:1-19 (see also Matt 15:1-20).
8 Matt 5:10, 23:1-36, Mk 12:38-40, Lk 11:37-52.

fell under the influence of false prophets and wicked kings. Well, the Pharisees weren't going to let that happen again on their watch! They knew exactly what the law demanded to be done with false prophets.

You killed false prophets.[9]

(And the Pharisees—by means of the Romans—did just that.)

Yet when Jesus himself spoke about the law, he never told people to abandon it. Jesus did, however, make grand and mysterious claims:

> *"Do not think that I have come to abolish the Law or the Prophets; I have not come to abolish them but to fulfill them."*[10]

Jesus embodied the deepest meaning and purpose of God's law.

And he was crystal clear about its ultimate intent:

> *"'Love the Lord your God with all your heart and with all your soul and with all your mind.' This is the first and greatest commandment. And the second is like it: 'Love your neighbor as yourself.' All the Law and the Prophets hang on these two commandments."*[11]

Jesus summarized the heartbeat of the Torah by quoting from the the Torah itself. And he also exposed the horrifying hypocrisy of those who claimed to understand the law but who failed to grasp its supreme purposes—justice and mercy and love.[12]

The law meant loving Yahweh
and loving other people.

---

9 Deut 18:20.
10 Matt 5:17.
11 Matt 22:37-40 (Mk 12:28-34) quoting Deut 6:4 and Lev 19:18.
12 Contrast the emphatic words of Jesus in Matt 9:13 and 12:7 with his criticism of the Pharisees in 23:13-36 (especially 23:23).

Love is the ultimate
meaning and purpose
of God's law.

This requires further exploration, because often when we read the earliest parts of the Bible—the book of the law—"love" doesn't immediately jump to mind. So much of it seems archaic and backwards to us. I mean, what are we to make of these dietary restrictions, cultural taboos and purity codes?

While we don't have space to engage all questions here,[13] one step in the right direction is to remember that God gave the Israelites these ancient cultural practices to give them space. To help craft them into a holy nation full of love and light in the midst of a savage and dark world. The nations of Egypt, Canaan, Assyria, Babylon and all the rest were not exactly known for their loving, hospitable or wholesome cultures. In fact, they frequently celebrated violence, injustice and power by brute force.

The parts of the law that seem exceptionally strange to us actually established strong cultural fences which kept Israel separate *from* the nations so they could shine a light *for* the nations.

You often need fences for gardens to grow.

But Israel became obsessed with itself. When will the kingdom of Yahweh come about *for them*? How can they finally be on top? They became obsessed with their national fence instead of regrowing Eden. The law became understood legalistically for the supremacy of Israel at the expense of the nations.

---

[13] For wrestling through some of the strangeness of the law and the Old Testament in general, I would recommend *Is God a Moral Monster* by Paul Copan (Grand Rapids: BakerBooks, 2011) and *God Behaving Badly* by David Lamb (Downsers Grove, IL: IVP, 2011).

But Jesus condemned this nationalistic, self-centered obedience.

His followers must be more upright than the Pharisees.[14] He blasted those who kept tiny details of the law while neglecting the redeeming love and justice behind it.[15] He told hellish stories of judgment against those who assumed themselves to be "in" and "blessed," challenging them to think and live differently.[16]

He called them to live lives truly honoring Yahweh.
He invited them to live lives of true love.

And living lives of true love would mean loving more than just caring for those who are good Torah-keeping Jews. More than loving those who think and act and believe the "right things." They must stop asking "who is the neighbor that I must love" and simply become loving neighbors.[17] They must even love the foreign oppressors that rule over them—they must love their enemies.[18]

But nobody should have been using any sort of religious law (especially the Torah) as an excuse not to love across boundaries, customs and religions. These things were precisely the point of the law. Yahweh gave the law with the intention that his people would bless the world. And, naturally, he still intends the same.

Jesus calls his disciples to be lovers.

14 Matt 5:20, which is a central theme through the entire book of Matthew.
15 Matt 23:13-28, Lk 11:39-52.
16 Matt 25:31-46, Lk 16:19-31 (see v14 for the setting of this story). It is interesting how these stories have often been used as harsh evidences for eternal judgment by those who are religiously devout yet unloving. It is Pharisees these judgments were spoken against.
17 Lk 10:25-37.
18 Matt 5:46-48; Lk 6:32-38.

The way his disciples love and bless the world will be the way you can recognize them.[19] The Pharisees were correct, Jesus did challenge many of the cultural aspects of Israel's law. But he also actually made other areas tougher, because he aimed straight at the hateful habits of the heart.[20]

And his earliest followers caught it. Jesus called them to obey the law at the deepest possible level. So the early church loved across barriers with incredible ferocity. It had finally clicked:

Love is the fulfillment of the law.[21]

When this clicks for us, it revolutionizes our thinking in at least two ways. First, we realize that God himself actually fulfills the law. He did this in Jesus through his sacrificial and love-driven death.[22]

> *Whoever does not love does not know God, because God is love. This is how God showed his love among us: He sent his one and only Son into the world that we might live through him. This is love: not that we loved God, but that he loved us and sent his Son as an atoning sacrifice for our sins. Dear friends, since God so loved us, we also ought to love one another.*[23]

The law can fully shape our lives—we can live as lovers—since the law has been fulfilled by the Lover of lovers.[24]

Jesus walked in obedient trust to Yahweh.

And he didn't miss a step.
He loved with every breath.

---

19 Jn 13:34-35, 15:17.
20 e.g. Matt 5:20-48.
21 Rom 13:10b (see also Gal 5:13-14 & Ja 2:8).
22 Rom 8:3-4.
23 1 Jn 4:8-11.
24 Rom 10:4.

And now we love because he loved us first.[25]

It's possible to love. Because this Lover's Spirit has invaded us.[26]

Second, love fulfilling the law recalibrates our understanding of what it means to break the law. That is, what it means "to sin." Many in the church talk about **"sin"** as something arbitrary and abstract. We talk about sin as if it's something detached and depersonalized. We become consumed with questions like: "Is *this* a sin?" or "When does *that* become a sin?"

But perhaps there are better questions we should ask.

Because sin is never arbitrary.
It's never abstract or depersonalized.

Hear this, God never simply just came up with rules on some kind of cosmic chalkboard. He wasn't just flipping a coin. It's not like he posted a "one-way street" sign that might just as well have gone the other direction. Sin really seems downright silly when we think of it as arbitrary, abstract and depersonalized.

But when God points us toward love, he's pointing us to the very fabric of the universe. Because he himself is love.[27] The very essence of the universe is loving. We're talking about a river, not a one-way street. Creation goes one direction because that's its nature—it's hardwired with its Creator's DNA.

Sin—on the other hand— fights against this current.

---

25 1 Jn 4:19.
26 1 Jn 4:12-17.
27 1 Jn 4:16b.

Hatred tears at the very fabric of reality.

Every broken commandment breaks a heart.
Every violation of the law is a violation of love.

This is one basic way of understanding ethics in the light of Jesus.

We are learning to reflect the Image of God which is love.

Love—that Image that gives the cosmos its shape.
Love—that Glue that holds the entire universe together.
Love—that Foundation undergirding all of reality.

Perhaps our questions should weigh whether our hearts and actions are in harmony with the heartbeat of love pumping through the universe.

Because every sin is ultimately a blood clot.

When we reframe it this way, of course we must love one another. How else can we reflect his Image? This is why loving one another is emphasized in the New Testament. It's the way we properly orbit the Center of the Universe. The "love chapter" read commonly during weddings is actually aimed at orienting the entire church, not merely marriages.[28] Because communities of Jesus are to be communes of love.

All we've got to do is love? It's that simple?
Yes, that's all we've got to do. Yes, it's that simple.

---

[28] Paul's addressing of marriage came in 1 Cor 7:1-16 and 1 Cor 13 is dealing with the community serving each other with its gifts. This, of course, does not mean that it does not speak into marriages, but marriages are not primarily in view. Thanks to Richard Hays, *Moral Vision of the New Testament*, 35 for pointing this out.

But what do we mean by "love"?

We can never make love something cheap or trivial. Or uncostly.

In the English language, the word "love" means almost nothing because we use it for so many different things. We love hotdogs and love our spouse in the same minute. So when we talk about "love," we must allow Scripture to define what exactly we're talking about. The "love" which we —as communities and individuals—are meant to be living is not spineless, flimsy, relativistic or undisciplined.

The word "love"
must be defined
by Jesus.

Love is defined by the self-giving obedience of the cross.[29]

Love is giving ourselves over for the good of others. It's not a feeling and definitely doesn't always feel good. In fact, sacrificial self-giving is often excruciating. But our King instructs us to embrace giving up our lives for both his sake and for the sake of others. We are to seek the good of others and the goodness of God's kingdom especially when we don't feel like it.

And as we define "love," we must not mistake it with pleasantries or politeness. We must look to the Jesus who turned over tables in the face of corruption,[30] who was angry in the presence of hard-heartedness[31] and who spoke concretely about truth[32] while giving himself up for

---

[29] Jn 15:13, 1 Jn 3:16.
[30] Matt 21:12-17, Mk 11:12-21, Lk 19:45-48, Jn 2:13-25.
[31] Mk 3:1-6.
[32] Jn 14:5-21.

others.[33] His entire life, he was acting in self-giving service for the good of the world.

This is love.

There's nothing cheap, trivial or uncostly about it.
And there's nothing weak or timid about it.

Our King, the Lover of lovers, fulfilled the law of love himself.

And his Spirit invades those willing, so we can be lovers who live in harmony with the heartbeat of the universe.

Which is another way of saying
we begin to taste true humanity.

---

[33] Matt 10:28, Mk 10:45.

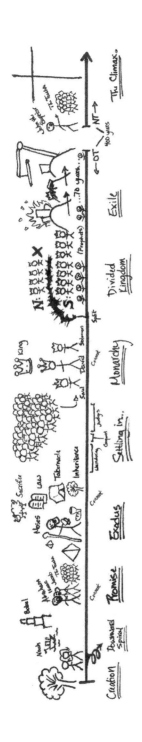

19 truly human

As the Bible's story opened, God created human beings unique among creation—they were crafted from the dust as creatures "in-God's-own-image." These dearly loved dirt-people would embody his very heart. And he purposed that that humanity would reflect his image in both responsibility and relationship—working the garden and ruling creation in community.

This is the way human life was designed.
This is what it means to be truly human.

But we—the walking dirt—wanted to live a different way.

We wanted to tell a different story than the one God was telling.

We wanted to be gods, making our own rules.
We wanted to chart our own self-sufficient way.

So instead of ruling the garden, we chose exile from it. God sang light into existence but we chose darkness. And our lives became a shadow of what God intended. The damage done *by* humanity was also done *to* humanity:

Shame and rebellion shattered relationships and communities.
Selfishness smothered intimacy, making our lives small.

We became darkened, rebelling against our Creator's heart instead of reflecting it.

And even the family of Abraham—whom Yahweh chose to be a blessing to the world—frequently and willfully brought more darkness to the story than light.[1] Israel was meant to show the Creator's design. To be the people that put on display humanity's true purposes. A kingdom of priests. A holy nation.

Yet over and over, Israel proved itself incapable of reflecting the image of the good Creator to the world.[2] Those who were elected to bless the world seemed absolutely powerless to obey Yahweh, despite their sometimes sincere intentions.[3]

Humanity's desperate and darkened plight was not lost on the earliest followers of Jesus. In a letter to an early church in Rome, Paul explores this inability of humanity (and specifically Israel) to live as God intended. He eventually resolves that Israel could not possibly live as a holy people —could not possibly follow Yahweh's commands—because a rebellious selfishness had infected all of humanity too deeply.[4]

Darkness had spread through all of us.
Corruption plunged its venomous roots deep.

God, in his grace, made us the walking dirt,
but sin left us the walking dead.

We traded worshipping God for worshipping creation—the material world, other people and ourselves. And the all-powerful Creator

---

[1] Israel is a case study for how humanity rebels early and often. For examples, see Ex 32 and 1 Kings 12:25-33.
[2] Ex 19:5-6 and Lev 19:1
[3] e.g. Deut 26:17 is followed quickly by 31:16; and Josh 24:14-18 is followed quickly by 24:19-20.
[4] Rom 7:7-25.

considers our choices to be so important that he gave us over to what we wanted. Humanity (Israel included) was so given over to darkness—so dehumanized—that we couldn't think rightly (much less live) rightly.[5]

We cut ourselves off from the source of all meaning, order, justice, beauty and hope. We cut ourselves off from the Author of Life.

This human addiction to rebellion was obvious to the earliest Christians. We grasp for more and more of everything—trying to feel better about our lives of walking death. We just want to feel something. Anything. But the more we claw and grasp for what we think will bring us life on our own terms, the emptier we become.[6]

Lives of rebellion against God's image are less-than-human lives.

But God did not desert his darkened, disintegrating dirt-people.
He would have the walking dead be fully alive and truly human.

The fourth gospel gives us a glimpse of the hope of new creation. By echoing Genesis, John signals the kind of story he's going to be telling. Genesis told the story of creation, and now John's telling the story of New Creation.[7] The coming of Jesus is the return of the Creator's purposes.

In him was life, and that life was the light of all mankind. The light shines in the darkness, and the darkness has not overcome it... The true light that gives light to everyone was coming into the world.[8]

---

5 Rom 1:18-32.
6 Eph 4:17-19 describes how our rebellion ultimately leads to insatiable selfishness.
7 Jn 1:1.
8 Jn 1:4-5, 9.

The earliest Christians told the story of the God who created light—the God who *is* Light—who also plunged into the midst of his darkened people. And he did this to bring new creation through judgment. The story of God recreating humanity by becoming human.

This thread in the fourth gospel comes into sharp focus during Jesus' trials. Pilate parades Jesus before the crowd and ironically (and prophetically!) announces: *"Here is the man!"*[9]

Could John's masterful style make the point any more strongly?
The Light of all mankind has become the True Human.
Yahweh has put on display what Israel could not—true humanity.[10]

The terrifying tragedy of John's gospel is that the leaders of Israel refused to recognize the Man actually embodying what they were designed to be. Worse, the walking dead crucified the true Image of God.[11]

This crucifixion, however, had divine purpose. John understands Jesus' death as the moment when the long-awaited judgment of the world actually happened. Mysteriously, Jesus brought that cosmic moment into the present through the cross.[12]

The Good Judge finally dealt with rebellion and darkness, both in the world "out there" and in our hearts "in here." The gavel fell. Judgment was rendered. And this judgment restores our truest humanity.

---

9 Jn 19:5b.
10 This would later be clearly articulated by the Church at the council of Chalcedon in 451 AD: "[Jesus] is perfect in Godhead and perfect in manhood, very God and very man."
11 Jn 1:18, 2 Cor 4:4b, Col 1:15, Heb 1:3.
12 e.g Jn 3:16-21, 36; 12:30-33, 47-48.

God became the True Man so we could once again become truly human —truly reflecting our Creator's image.[13] Or in the words of John:

> He came to that which was his own, but his own did not receive him. Yet to all who did receive him, to those who believed in his name, he gave the right to become children of God—children born not of natural descent, nor of human decision or a husband's will, but born of God.[14]

In his life, Jesus gave an example of the truly human life.[15]
In his death, Jesus creates a new humanity.[16]

We have already heard the call to repent—the call to change—as Jesus' invitation to exodus. The new and true humanity created in Jesus is the reason why Christians heed that call. On our own, we are disfigured, disintegrating rebels. But when we trust Jesus, we are invaded by his Spirit[17] and transformed into his image as we walk in humble submission to him.[18]

Transformed into the Image we were always meant to reflect.[19]
Into the Image that makes us human.
We become what we were always meant to be.

But much to our frequent resistance, this transformation takes us down a surprising path to a surprising destination.

It takes us through suffering to service.

In other words, our lives begin to look a lot like the cross.

---

13 See Irenaeus, *Against Heresies*, III, 19 1.
14 Jn 1:11-13.
15 1 Pet 2:21.
16 Eph 2:15b.
17 Eph 1:13 (cf. Rom 8:14-17, 2 Cor 1:22, Gal 4:4-7).
18 1 Cor 15:49, 2 Cor 3:16-18, Gal 5:16-26.
19 Eph 4:20-24, Col 3:5-10.

First, **suffering** is not at all what we would have planned. It's definitely not the kind of advertising many Western mega-churches employ.[20] Jesus is not primarily interested in giving us a booster-shot of self-esteem or material prosperity. Jesus is calling us to abandon our self-centered and self-serving self-sufficiency. Jesus calls us to take up a cross and follow him.[21]

Jesus is interested in killing us.

Paul actually declares that (mystery of mysteries) he himself had actually died with Jesus on the cross, and God himself had taken up residence within him.[22] For him, embracing the death of the cross is simply embracing what had already happened.

C.S. Lewis once imagined Jesus talking in this way:

> "Give me All. I don't want so much of your time and so much of your money and so much of your work: I want You. I have not come to torment your natural self, but to kill it. No half-measures are any good. I don't want to cut off a branch here and a branch there, I want to have the whole tree down. I don't want to drill the tooth, or crown it, or stop it, but to have it out. Hand over the whole natural self, all the desires which you think innocent as well as the ones you think wicked—the whole outfit. I will give you a new self instead. In fact, I will give you Myself: my own will shall become yours."[23]

Having the whole tree down (or the tooth out) means embracing a life shaped by the cross. A lifetime of relentlessly remembering reality—we died with Jesus on the cross. And this *will* often be excruciatingly painful.

---

20 The church sign or website could read: "Come to our church and learn how to die!"
21 Matt 16:24, Mk 8:34b, Luke 8:23b.
22 Gal 2:20.
23 C.S. Lewis, *Mere Christianity* (New York: Harper Collins, 2001), 196-197.

But to be a Christian is to cling so tightly to Jesus that we participate in the redemptive suffering of the cross.[24]

We relearn what it means to be human through the way of the cross. It's one of the primary ways that God's Spirit teaches us that the universe is good and beautiful and not all about us. We learn to detox from selfishness and see beyond ourselves. We learn to trust that the God who raised Jesus from the dead will raise us from the dead.

Now this is definitely not the sort of thing that I would have made up. I would have made up a religion that promises me health and wealth and everything that I want—all I have to "sow" (donate) some sort of "seed" (money) to the number on the screen. But that would just be a monstrous manipulation of Scripture that furthers my own selfishness.[25]

The fact that I wouldn't have put suffering at the center of my worldview actually comforts me. The Christ-centered worldview addresses the world in bigger ways than anything I could have dreamt up. One theologian describes it this way:

> The way of the cross is often misunderstood as masochistic, especially in an age so desperately in search of pleasure. But the suffering of which Jesus spoke is not the suffering that unwell people create for themselves. Instead, it is the suffering already present in the world, which we can either identify with or ignore. If pain were not real, if it were not the lot of so many, the way of the cross would be pathological. But in our world—with its millions of hungry, homeless, and hopeless people—it is pathological to live as if pain did not exist. The way of the cross means allowing that pain to carve one's life into a channel through which the healing stream of the spirit can flow to a world in need.[26]

---

24 In 2 Cor 4:6-18, Paul talks about his suffering in terms of healing and rescue for others. (See also Col 1:24, where Paul talks about making redemption visible for others since they didn't see Jesus die.)
25 If you missed it, that was a jab at television "theology" which is damaging countless lives.
26 Parker Palmer, *The Promise of Paradox* (San Francisco: Jossey-Bass, 1993) , 32-33.

God always offers us a choice. We can choose the redemptive, transformative suffering of the cross or the meaningless suffering of selfishness.

But a life devoid of suffering is not an option.

In the midst of our often pain-filled lives, we can have confidence that God is transforming us more and more into his image when we center ourselves on the cross. As we pursue Jesus, suffering is actually evidence that God's Spirit is present, working and renewing us.[27] Instead of despair in struggle, we can (and should) rejoice—as strange or difficult or impossible as that may seem at times.[28] Nothing will be wasted.[29] God transforms the trusting and the humble into his image through their crosses.

But even more, our **joy** comes from knowing that we are actually following a path blazed by God himself. The True Man reconciled the world back to God through his suffering.[30] Unavoidable, undeniable suffering fills the world, so it is deeply comforting to know that there really is such a thing as redemptive suffering.

There can and will be "purpose to our pain"
when we trust, embrace, and follow the crucified God.[31]

But our transformation is not merely for us. The True Human shows us that we are meant to be servants. We're meant to pouring ourselves out for each other:

---

27 1 Pet 4:14.
28 Rom 5:3-5, 2 Cor 11:18-12:10, Ja 1:2-4.
29 Rom 8:18-30.
30 2 Cor 5:19.
31 Thanks to my dear friend John MacTaggart for this phrase.

So then, those who suffer according to God's will should commit themselves to their faithful Creator and continue to do good.[31]

In the garden, Adam and Eve greedily grabbed to be gods. But Jesus shows us what the true image of God looks like: humility that endures suffering for the sake of others. The all-powerful God of the universe is a humble servant who seeks the good of others.

No exaggeration. No hyperbole.
That's the scandal of the God-man's cross.[32]

And this is exactly why Jesus is worthy of worship—because he's so shockingly different than the types of gods we would be.

When Jesus calls us to **serve** one another, he's not telling us to do something foreign to himself. He's inviting us into the very life of the Divine—into what he himself already does. So we truly reflect this God's image most in humility. We become most truly human in service.

Have this mind in you that was also in King Jesus.[33]

As we detox through the cross, we begin glimpsing a bigger, more wondrous world than we imagined:

A world where we can finally shed the burden of selfishness.

A world where we are delightfully small.
A world where we can serve the other.

---

32 See the grand hymn of Phil 2:6-11. It's precisely the humility to suffer and serve that makes Jesus worthy of worship.
33 This is exactly the point of Phil 2:3-5—we are to be mirrors of Jesus' character both in his decision to become human and his decision to go to the cross. And seriously, no joke, you have permission to translate christos as "king."

At its best, the Church puts on display this new humanity. That is, after all, its very heart. At the heart of the two great mysteries of the Christian Church—baptism and the Lord's supper—we find signs of God, the suffering servant. Both of these ancient rituals ground the Church in the redemptive suffering of Jesus which ultimately serves and saves the world.

Entering the Christian community through baptism invokes the long, rich history of God rescuing his people through chaotic waters of death and bringing them safely into new life.[34] All the moments which were just early echoes of the cross.

Baptism is the act of accepting Jesus' death for ourselves. An acceptance that we too are embarking—along with the rest of the people of God—into the suffering of Jesus so that we can also participate in his resurrection.[35]

Likewise, the act of the Church centering herself around the table—around the bread and the cup—proclaims the death of Jesus until he returns to banish death from the world.[36]

Because Jesus is alive, remembering him as the broken Passover lamb is serious celebration. We stare unblinkingly into the face of pain, atrocity, sorrow, and death and recklessly proclaim that God is putting us back together in the midst of it. That our crosses are redemptive because of Jesus' resurrection.

Both baptism and the Lord's supper rituals meant to root us in the humble, suffering service of Jesus. Both acts commission the new

---

[34] 1 Pet 3:20-21 makes this symbolism explicit.
[35] See Rom 6:3-4 (and see too Rom 8:17b and Phil 3:10-11)
[36] 1 Cor 11:26.

humanity for its task of become suffering servants who reflect the image of the Suffering Servant.[37]

To participate with a God who brings purpose to our pain.
To serve each other in humility.

To celebrate being truly human.

And this is a new humanity that transcends everything that we find to divide ourselves. Humanity may have wandered away from the tower of Babel with our languages confused.[38] But when God poured out his Spirit at Pentecost, he was signaling that Babel's fracture had been reversed in Jesus. No babbling here. Through the Spirit of Jesus, we understand each other crystal clearly.[39]

Self-giving suffering service doesn't need translation.

So whatever divided us in the old humanity cannot divide us in the new. Race, gender, class and every other excuse we find to divide ourselves has been overridden and enveloped in Jesus.

This reality was just as difficult to embody in the first century as today. But whenever and wherever colonies of the new humanity are established, they must challenge any culture (be it religious, political or popular) that stereotypes, separates, polarizes or pigeonholes. When religious communities fall into these traps, something is desperately wrong, no matter what tops their steeple.

The reign of the Suffering Servant demands that we live united.[40]

---

37 Gal 6:9-10, Eph 2:8-10, Heb 10:24-25, 1 Pet 2:11-17, 4:19.
38 Gen 11:1-9.
39 Acts 2:2-12.
40 Gal 3:26-29; Col 3:11.

It's impossible to live as servants and live divided.

God has become the True Human who restores his image to everyone who will receive it. He unites the humble and the willing as the new humanity who serve each other—especially through our suffering. We are finally relearning what it means to be human. What it means to live under the reign of the King.

Because Jesus really is King.
He really is Lord.

He really does live.
Today.

He really does reign over the universe.
Today.

His kingdom has budded.
New Creation is blossoming.

True life is beginning to bloom.
And one day the rose will open.

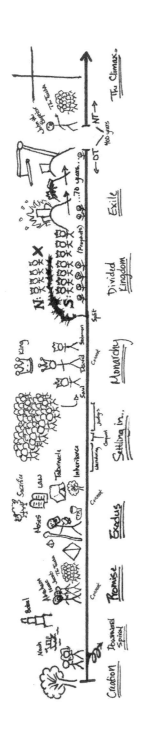

20 the inheritance

The Story of all stories began with a song. God created his creation and it was good, it was good, it was very good. In the beginning the Creator and his creation, heaven and earth, God and mankind—they were together. The Story ends in the same way—paradise restored.[1] Between the garden of delight and the city of delight, however, we learn much about God:

This Creator is not detached. He is also the Redeemer who loves his creation enough to not abandon it. In the tragedy of humanity's downward spiral, we discover the patience and relentless love of God in a way we may never have known otherwise.

This is a God who doesn't let go—who will restore paradise lost and regrows Eden in everyone that will permit him.

The longing to return to Eden emerges frequently in the Bible. As early as the promises to Abraham, we ache for the land we were made for— that lost land of Eden, brimming with rivers and gold.[2] Yahweh promised an inheritance of land to Abraham only precious chapters after humanity's original inheritance had been corrupted. He was promising a home-to-come to his people-to-come.

---

[1] Read Gen 1-2 and Rev 21-22 back-to-back.
[2] Gen 2:8-15.

The promise of land was about more than just land. That ache for Eden reminds us where this story has come from, and gives us glimpses of where it's going.

Tragically, Abraham's family did not keep their land for long. They were banished from the land because of their rebellion just as humanity was banished from Eden.

Humanity seemed destined to squander their inheritance.

Yet the prophets who emerged during and after Israel's exile envisioned a day when the land—and even Eden itself—would finally be restored. Isaiah, for example, declares:

> The LORD will surely comfort Zion and will look with compassion on all her ruins; he will make her deserts like Eden, her wastelands like the garden of the LORD. Joy and gladness will be found in her, thanksgiving and the sound of singing.[3]

Israel's return from exile anticipates a truer and deeper day—the Day when humanity itself will return from its exile from Eden. But this return of Eden would require an act of judgment to finally obliterate darkness from creation.

The Bible is not spineless—it speaks strongly about the goodness of God, the rebellion of man and the world's need for **judgement**. Just as God showed himself a Judge who must destroy evil in the story of Noah, so too the prophets also reiterated the need for evil to be purged. They condemned corruption, violence and idolatry with often incredibly strong and vivid language.[4]

---

[3] Isaiah 51:3 (e.g. see also the imagery in Ezk 36:33-36, Joel 3:17-21, Amos 9:13-15).

[4] You can take your pick of plenty of condemnations from prophets. Examples include Isa 13-24; Jer 8--9, Ezk 4-16, Hosea 4-10, Amos 1-6.

These condemnations and judgments can disturb us. But surely we would be more disturbed if they weren't there. After all, the undeniable evil that fills the world then (and now!) makes us all yearn for a Judge who can—and will!—finally bring justice.

And so the prophets eagerly anticipated Yahweh becoming King and judging the earth. That would be a day that all the universe could finally celebrate.[5]

When judgment came, it would be incredible news for the world.

Someone would set things right.

The terrifying reality, however, is that we ourselves are part of the problem. We contribute to the evil of the world. We participate in it. So when judgment comes, it will be terrible news for us.

We all long for a Judge,
but we ourselves must be judged.

So one of the glories of the earliest Christian proclamation was that somehow the judgment of all the evil in the world took place on the cross.[6] They insisted that—in Jesus—Yahweh had become not only the world's King but also the world's Judge.[7]

And the hysterically good news is what sort of Judge he is.

Jesus is the Judge who judged himself in our place.[8]

---

[5] e.g. Ps 47:1-9, 96:10-13; Isa 2:2-5.
[6] e.g. Rom 8:3-4.
[7] e.g. Jn 8:16; Acts 10:44, 17:31; Rom 2:16, 14:10-12; 2 Cor 5:10; 2 Tim 4:1; 1 Pet 4:5.
[8] Karl Barth, Church Dogmatics, IV, 1.

More jaw-dropping than God becoming man is the character of this God. He has revealed himself as the Judge willing to take all the violence, evil and injustice of the world onto himself. So Christians are those who entrust themselves to the judgment of the cross and the character of the Judge. And when they do this, they discover they are acquitted—they are not condemned.[9]

And the news gets better. Those willing to embrace this Judge's verdict discover they have been adopted as dearly loved children—heirs of an embarrassingly excessive inheritance.[10] Those who trust God like Abraham enter into his family and are promised an inheritance—the entire world.[11]

Jesus is the good Judge who manages to sign both a well-deserved death penalty and utterly undeserved adoption papers.[12]

Not guilty.
Adopted. Heir.
Inheritance.

This is the verdict rendered for those willing to trust the Judge.

As hard as it may be to believe some days, there really is a coming Day when the inheritance will be given. When the land will be received. When hope for Eden's return will finally be rewarded because the judgment of the cross will purge all of reality.

We should say a few things with confidence about this coming inheritance—about the final blossoming of New Creation. First, the

9 Jn 3:16-21.
10 Rom 8:14-17, Gal 4:4-7.
11 Rom 4:13-16.
12 Rom 3:21-26.

"where" of New Creation. Many Christian traditions have mistakenly taught that the entire material world will be destroyed in fire and that our "inheritance" is some fuzzy, cloudy place out there called "heaven." Maybe somewhere with clouds and harps. Definitely something "out there" and away from here.

But "somewhere else" is not the grand vision of the Bible.[13]

Yes, those who die trusting Jesus find themselves in his presence and safe with him.[14] We tend to think of this "safe-with-Jesus-place" as the final destination. But this place receives very little attention in the Bible. In fact, we know much less about this immediate "safe-with-Jesus-place" than we know about what eventually comes after it.

Life after life after death.[15]

The entire biblical story points to the coming Day when all of creation will be restored and recreated. Death, destruction, darkness, rebellion and all the rest will finally be destroyed once and for all.[16] This picture is not of a disembodied, ambiguous or fuzzy world somewhere else. This is our world. Restored. And more real than anything we can imagine.
Jesus certainly has gone to prepare a place for us, but the "where" that he's preparing is not "out there."[17] He's preparing for the day when all creation is made new.

---

13 The confusion comes from a misreading of 2 Pet 3:5-12 that thinks of the earth as something that will be burnt up and discarded. This reading leaves out 3:13 which definitely affirms the rest of the Bible in its vision of restored universe. The imagery of fire is not divine arson but rather a purifying judgment like 1 Cor 3:10-15.
14 e.g. Lk 23:43, 2 Cor 5:8-10.
15 A phrase coined (I believe) by N.T. Wright in his fine book *Surprised by Hope* (New York: HarperOne, 2008). Add this book to the top of your list if this subject interests you.
16 Rev 20:11-15.
17 Jn 14:2-3.

One pastor put it this way:
"Heaven is where God is storing the earth's future."[18]

Indeed—that is where the Bible's story ends.

All things restored. **New Creation.**

Heaven comes to earth.[19]
God marries his humanity.[20]

That last sentence is telling and illuminates the "who" of New Creation. We must talk here about "his humanity" because the Bible indicates that some of humanity refuse to let God sweep them off their feet.

And God will only marry those who will have him.

Jesus is the bridegroom not a bride-napper.

This is our final example of the ultimate power of God and the true freedom of people—and there is plenty of tension here:

God is sovereign—he'll have his way in the end with creation being remade and humankind restored to his image. And there are a staggering number of passages in the Bible indicating that God truly desires for every single person to be a part of that wedding celebration.[21] The Creator didn't make anyone he simply wants to scrap—he really does long for every last person who has ever existed to choose obedience, humility and life over rebellion, arrogance and death.[22]

---

18 Rob Bell in his preaching lecture series, "Prophets, Preachers, and Poets."
19 Isa 65:17-25, Rev 21:1-4.
20 Eph 5:31-32, Rev 19:6-9.
21 e.g. Ezk 18:32, 33:11; Rom 5:18-19, 11:25-32; 1 Cor 15:21-22; Phil 2:10-11; Col 1:15-20; 1 Tim 2:1-4, 4:10; Titus 2:11, 2 Pet 3:9.
22 Deut 30:15, 19.

But some willfully and continually reject his marriage proposal.

They refuse the wooing of life
and insist on an existence of death.

They will tragically be doomed to die like death itself.[23]

But those desperate, humble, and willing enough to trust the resurrected
Jesus will themselves be resurrected like him.[24]

This is where many popular conceptions of heaven actually distort and
distract. We are absolutely not talking about disembodied souls floating
around in clouds. We're talking about real people resurrected with real
bodies in a real world.[25]

These aren't floaty, fuzzy souls;
they're complete, whole, real, solid people.

This is creation and humanity as they were meant to be. For Christians,
the future should never be imagined as less real, less majestic or less
creative than what we know now.

The fate of humanity has sometimes been imagined as lounging around
with harps or—in more popular (and scary) Christian imagination—
singing "worship music" forever! But these pictures fail to fit Scripture's
story leading us to the New Eden. God's not going to jettison his intent
for creation in favor of some sort of never-ending church service. Any
kind of existence without the real work, real responsibility, and real

---

23 1 Cor 6:9-10, Gal 5:19-21, Eph 5:5, Rev 21:7-8.
24 Jn 11:25-26, Rom 8:23, Phil 3:20-21, 1 Jn 3:2-3.
25 This is the entire argument of the incredible 1 Cor 15. The only place we find souls in heaven with no
bodies is in Rev 6:9-11, and in that passage these souls are not eternally and blissfully happy. Rather
they are waiting and longing and crying out for the resurrection and for God's justice to fill and restore
the entire earth.

relationships of God's creation would more accurately be called "hell" than "heaven."

It would be a less-than-human-existence;
less than what God intended from the beginning.

Our imaginations must try to do justice to the Bible's vision.

I think we're on safe ground when we imagine
new discoveries in new lands,
new architecture in new climates,
new music with new instruments,
new jokes with new words,
new stories with new plots,
new gardening with new plants,
new recipes with new ingredients,
and new art with new colors.

New Creation is more, not less.

All this is worship—and I don't doubt that we'll get together for concerts too. But we must try to picture people enjoying and worshiping God with full lives of building and planting, singing and celebrating, reigning and feasting.[26]

This is work without futility,
intimacy without shame,
community without conflict,
and life without death.

God will give the renewed cosmos to his adopted heirs.

---

[26] Isa 65: 21-22, Rev 22:5b.

Since New Creation will be wonderfully more than the present world—not less—our imaginations fail us at this point. Who can imagine this kind of world? The burden of death plagues our lives and stifles our imaginations to such an extent that we cannot properly imagine an existence rid of it.

We're shadows dreaming of solids.

In the closing lines of *The Chronicles of Narnia*, C.S. Lewis hints at this new world and leaves us haunted with unbridled hope:

> "There *was* a real railway accident," said Aslan softly. "Your father and mother and all of you are—as you used to call it in the Shadowlands—dead. The term is over: the holidays have begun. The dream is ended: this is the morning."
>
> And as He spoke He no longer look to them like a lion; but the things that began to happen after that were so great and beautiful that I cannot write them. And for us this is the end of all the stories, and we can most truly say that they all lived happily ever after. But for them it was only the beginning of the real story. All their life in this world and all their adventures in Narnia had only been the cover and the title page: now at last they were beginning Chapter One of the Great Story which no one on earth has read: which goes on forever: in which every chapter is better than the one before.[27]

This life, this world, this universe, is beautiful. And all of it points us to our crucified and resurrected God, who is beautiful.

So let us live lives worthy of the story that we find ourselves in:

Let us pledge our allegiance to the King of the universe who rightfully reclaims every square inch of reality for himself.

---

[27] C.S. Lewis, *The Last Battle* (New York: Harper Collins, 1994), 210-211. This book is one of the most moving imaginings of new creation that I've ever read.

Let us proclaim the faithfulness of our Creator and how he fulfills all of his promises even when it means sacrifice.

Let us dare to declare that the powers of corruption and rebellion, evil and injustice, death and the devil have been conquered.

Let us trust again and again that we have been gripped by grace for the good of the world.

Let us celebrate how the unfathomable God of the universe remains closer to us than any of us dare to dream.

Let us keep in step with his Spirit who transforms us into the lovers and suffering servants we were always meant to be.

And let us stand firm as we hope for our coming inheritance—the day when we will embrace our Creator, laugh with our Redeemer, feast with our Bridegroom. When we will worship our God, serve each other, and reign with him forever. World without end.

Come, Lord Jesus.
The grace of the Lord Jesus be with God's people.
Amen.[28]

---

[28] Rev 22:20b-21.

last words

I'm not sure that the "acknowledgments" of a book can possibly mean much to most readers. But having gone through the grueling process of writing this, I definitely have a new appreciation for this section. It's really for me and those around me. This would never have gotten written without the love, support and encouragement of those around me—I cannot thank anyone enough.

I am absolutely indebted to the scholarship and pastoral heart of N.T. Wright. I cannot possibly tell you how enlightening and inspiring I have found his work and his ministry. I've digested so much of his work that this entire book deserves a footnote with his name under it.[1]

I've also had wind put in my sails and been given my bearings through the work of C.S. Lewis, G.K. Chesterton, Karl Barth, Dietrich Bonhoeffer, Eugene Peterson, Richard Hays, John Goldingay and Scot McKnight. These men are giants—which is to say, they are servants. I thank them.

Now for those people I've actually met. Mike Garrett didn't laugh when I suggested writing this in fall 2010—he fanned this project's flame when it was merely an ember. Ashley, Marsha and Bolin Phipps labored intimately with me, reading (atrocious) early drafts of chapters and insisting that the project was not a fool's errand. My family (especially my mother and twin brother) gave me copious grammatical and content suggestions after the second draft. My archenemy Adam marked up the third draft in a similar fashion, and sweet Connie Wennen did the same on the final draft. You all have been incredibly patient and offensively underpaid editors. Thank you, thank you, thank you.

---

[1] See the collected works of N.T. Wright. There, I feel better.

Countless friends—like Aaron Eldridge, John MacTaggart, Chris Culver, Kris Broadhead, Micah and Heather Simpson, Ryan Smothers, Adam Oliver, Aaron and Diana Ashlock, Stephanie Davis, Christy Averill, Mike Lewis and Joy Wennen—breathed life into me during the writing, editing and polishing process with their feedback and encouraging words. I'm not exaggerating—this wouldn't have gotten done without you.

It's impossible to list all the friends who spoke (and speak) life into me.

You know who you are—thank you. Really.

The communities of Mosaic Birmingham, Beeson Divinity School and The Church at Ross Bridge provided me shelter in storms and continuous guidance.

Above all, I thank you, Jesus. Please, show yourself as great through this, build your Church, tell your story and teach me faith, love, and hope.

APPENDIX: CHEAT SHEET

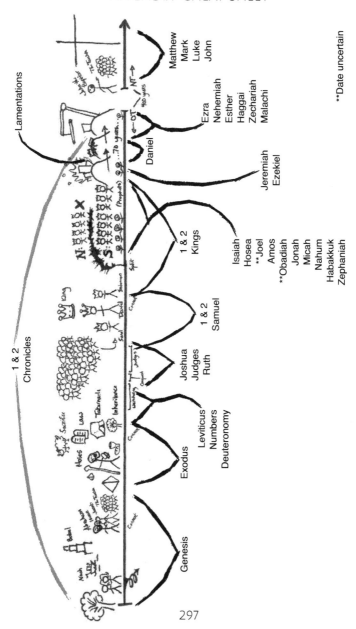

Genesis

Exodus
Leviticus
Numbers
Deuteronomy

Joshua
Judges
Ruth

1 & 2
Samuel

1 & 2
Kings

Isaiah
Hosea
**Joel
Amos
**Obadiah
Jonah
Micah
Nahum
Habakkuk
Zephaniah

Jeremiah
Ezekiel

Daniel

Ezra
Nehemiah
Esther
Haggai
Zechariah
Malachi

Matthew
Mark
Luke
John

Lamentations

1 & 2
Chronicles

**Date uncertain

GENESIS

1:1	247
1:1-3	251
1:1-5	163
1:2-3	22
1:3	23, 247
1:9	22
1:12	22
1:18	22
1:21	22
1:25	22
1:26	251
1:27	23, 26
1:28	23, 41, 50
1:28-29	40
1:31	24
1—2	284
2:1-3	23
2:4	25, 159
2:7	26
2:8-15	26, 284
2:10-14	37
2:15-16	26
2:16-17	27, 32
2:17	35
2:18	28
2:23	28
2:25	29
3—11	32
3:1-24	24
3:6	33, 39
3:8	79
3:12	36
3:14	37
3:14-19	213
3:15b	37
3:16	37
3:16a	50
3:16b	37
3:17-18	37
3:18	196
3:19	38
3:20	38
4:1-8	38
4:1-12	205
4:9b	38
4:10	38, 207
4:17-26	39
4:23-24	39
5	39
5:1	25, 161
6:5	39
6:9	39
6:9—9:17	40
8:21	40
9:1	41, 50
9:1-7	40
9:7	50
10	46
10:1	25, 159
11	46
11:1	42
11:1-9	41, 280
11:4	41
11:5	41
11:7	41
11:9	42
11:10	25, 159
11:27	47
11:30	50
12:2	208, 230
12:2-3	47, 193
12:11-16	51
15	75
15:5	48
15:6	51
15:7	48
16:1-4	51
17:5	46
17:6-7	193
17:8	48
17:9-14	48
17:15	46
18	251
18:9-15	50
18:18	193, 208, 230
20:1-2	51
21:1-20	51
22:1-19	52, 205
22:8	52
22:12	120
22:17-18	193
22:18	208, 230
25:21	52
25:24-26	53
25:29-34	54
27:1-40	54
27:41	54
28:13-14	54
28:20-22	55
29:15-30	55
30:25-43	55
32:22-32	56
35:9-15	56

GENESIS (Cont.)

37:1—47:12 57
49:10 193
50:20 57

EXODUS

1:1-7 60
1:8 60
1:9 61
1:10 61
1:12b-14 61
1:15-16 219
1:16 62
1:22 62
2:3, 5 62
2:5-10 62
2:11-15 62
2:16-22 62
2:23 208
3:1 72
3:1-10 63
3:14-15 245
3:16-17 65
3:19 66
3:22b 67
4:11 63
4:12 63
4:27 72
4:21 66
4:22 ....66, 162
7:3 67
7:13 67
7:14—12:30 66
7:23 67
8:15 67
8:19 67
8:32 67
9:7 67
9:12 67
9:34 67
10:20 67
10:27 67
11:1-8 65
11:10 67
12:1-30 ....66, 211
12:8-11 66
12:13 66
12:36 67
12:38 67
12:40-42 60
12:48-49 67
13:20-22 68
14:4 68
14:5 67
14:5-6 68
14:8 68

14:9 68
14:10-18 68
14:22 68
14:23-31 69
15 69
15:1 69
18:5 72
19:1 80
19:1-2 72
19:3-4 74
19:5-6 ....74, 232, 271
19:10-13 72
19:11 72
19:16-19 72
19:18 72
19:20 ....72, 73
20 168
20:1-17 74
20:2 74
20:4 120
24:3-8 77
24:8 181
24:13 77
25—30 79
32 271
32:1-6 77
32:15-20 78
32:30-35 78
32:31-32 218
33:3 79
33:5 79
34:5-7 245
36—40 79
40:34-35 116

LEVITICUS

1—7 ....80, 205
11—15 76
16 ....80, 205
                                                 209, 212
16:15-22 209
16:30 209
16:34 209
18:21 ....52, 120, 205
18:21-25 90
18:24-28 ....75, 132, 232
19:1 271
19:2 76
19:4 120
19:18 261
20:2-5 120
26:11-12 79

NUMBERS

1—4 80
1:1 80

NUMBERS (Cont.)

1:47-53	.80
6:22—7:89	.80
9:14	.80
9:15-23	.81
13:1-25	.81
13:26-33	.81
14:1-10a	.81
14:20-25	.81
14:34	.81
20:1-13	.84
21:1-3	.88
21:21-25	.90
22—24	.123
25:1-3	.97
27:12-23	.84
33:48-49	.82

DEUTERONOMY

1:5—4:10	.82
2:24—3:11	.88
5:1—26:15	.82
5:2	.72
5:8	.120
6:4	.197, 252, 261
6:4-6	.76
6:5	.83
6:13	.162
6:18	.162
7:7	.90
7:8	.90
7:12	.83
8:3	.162
8:22-28	.232
9:4-5	.91
9:6	.90
16:3	.181
18:15	.219
18:15-18	.84, 176, 178
18:18-19	.219
18:20	.261
20:16-18	.90
23:3	.97
26:17	.271
28	.131
28:1-14	.83
28:15-68	.83, 93 213, 232
28:64-68	.135
29:2—30:20	.82
30:1-6	.84, 136, 213
30:1-10	.233
30:9-10	.259
30:11-20	.232
30:15	.289
30:15-20	.83

30:19	.289
30:17-18	.74
31:1-8	.84
31:16	.271
31:17	.183
34:10-12	.84, 175

JOSHUA

1—12	.88
2:1-21	.92
1:6	.87
1:16-17	.87
3:1—5:1	.87
5:13—6:27	.88
6:20-25	.92, 93
7:1-26	.93
11:22a	.91
11:23b	.88
12:7-24	.88
13—24	.88
14:12-15	.91
15:13-14	.91
18:1	.103
21:43-45	.91
23:1	.88, 93
23:14	.91
23:15-16	.93
24:1-18	.93
24:14-18	.271
24:19-20	.271
24:19-24	.94
24:20	.93

JUDGES

1	.94
2:10-19	.95
3:12-30	.95
4:1-24	.95
6:1—8:35	.95
17:1—18:31	.96
17:6	.95
18:1	.96
18:27	.96
18:31	.103
19:1	.96
19:1-30	.96
19:30	.96
20:1-16	.96
20:17-48	.96
21:1-24	.96
21:25	.96

RUTH

General Info	.97-99
1:1	.99
4:22	.99

300

I SAMUEL

1:1-20 102
1:1—2:11 194
1:9 103
1:25-28 103
2:11 103
2:12 103
3:1a 103
3:1-18 104
3:20 104
4:1-18 104
4:18b 103
7:6b 104
7:13-14 104
7:15 104
8:1-5 105
8:5 105
8:7 106
8:9-22 106
9:1—10:8 106
9:1-2 106
9:15-16 107
10:1 123
10:9-11 106
10:9-26 106
10:17-27 107
13:6-14 107
13:13b-14 108
15:13-23 107
15:22 206
16:7b 108
16:13 .... 109, 123
16:14-23 109
17 109
18:10-11 109
19:9-10 109
20 109
20:16 231
21:10-15 109
23:18 231
24 109
26 109
31 110

II SAMUEL

1:17-27 110
2:1-7 110
5:1-4 110
5:6-10 110
7:1-2 110
7:11-16 .... 193, 196
7:11b-13 111
7:14 162
7:27 110
11 111
12:13-25 112

13:1-22 112
13:23-28 112
15—18 112

I KINGS

1 113
1:34 123
2:12 113
3:12-13 113
5:3-5 114
5:13-18 119
6 116
6:38—7:1 114
7:1-12 114
8:10-11 116
8:17-18 114
9:15-22 119
10:4 114
10:9b 119
10:14-25 119
10:26-29 119
11:4-8 120
11:9-13 120
12:16-24 120
12:25-33 .... 122, 271
14:14-16 126
16:23-24 121
17:1—II Kings 13:21 121
17:7-24 .... 124, 165
18:16-40 124
19:15-16 123
22:1-28 123
23:36—25:21 127

II KINGS

4:1-7 124
4:8-37 165
4:42-44 .... 124, 165
5:1-14 165
5:10-14 124
17 126
17:5-8 124
18—20 124
18:1—20:21 126
19:34 126
22:1—23:30 .... 121, 126
23:10 120
24:3 133
24:1-4 124
24:13 145
25:9 127
25:27-30 129

I CHRONICLES

General Info 141
3:19 145

I CHRONICLES (Cont.)
22:7-9 114

II CHRONICLES
General Info 141
7:14-18 259
36:20-23 141

EZRA
General Info 145
1:1-4 145
1:7 145
2:2 145
3:1-6 147
3:7-13 146
3:11-13 146
4:1-23 146
4:2 145
4:24 146
5:1-2 146
6:8 146
6:13-15 146
7:6-10 148
8:15-36 148
9—10 148
9:1—10:17 150
9:8-9 148

NEHEMIAH
General Info 145
1:1—2:10 148
4 148
6 148
6:15 148
8 148
9:36-37 148
13:23-27 150

ESTHER
General Info 151

JOB
General Info 140
1:8 140
1:22 140
2:3 140
2:9-10 140
31:1 231
38:8-11 168
42:7-17 140

PSALMS
General Info 114
2 162
2:7 161
8 33

18:50 193
19 259
22 183
47 197
47:1-9 286
49:7-9 213
50:7-15 206
89 23
89:3-4 193
89:11-15 90
89:19-37 162
96:10-13 286
110 196
119 259
130 248
132:10 193
137:1-4 128
145:10-13 197

PROVERBS
General Info 113
8:29 168

ECCLESIASTES
General Info 113

SONG OF SONGS
General Info 113

ISAIAH
General Info 136
1:10-25 123
1:11-17 206
2:2-5 286
6 165
11:1-9 260
13—24 285
20 124
25:7-8 196
26:19 186
33:22 197
40:3 136
40:6-8 247
40—66 136
42:1 162
45:1-14 141
45:23 197
49:6, 8-9 239
50:2 168
51:3 285
51:17-23 184
52—55 136
52:7 197
52:13—53:12 .... 136, 162, 211
53:5 213
55:7 167

55:10-11 247
65:17-25 .... 159, 202, 289
65:21-22 291

JEREMIAH
General Info 137
5:19 233
6:1-2 128
7:1-11 123
7:3-11 127
7:9-11 133
7:11 179
8—9 285
19 124
19:5 .... 52, 205
23:5-6 193
25:15-29 181
29:1-9 134
29:5-7 138
29:10 134
29:11 134
31:31-34 .... 78, 137
                                         181, 224, 233
31:35 168
32:25 120
33:14-17 193

LAMENTATIONS
General Info 128
3:21-33 128

EZEKIEL
General Info 137
4—5 124
4—16 285
8—11 153
9:3 148
10:18 148
11:23 148
16 137
16:59-63 .... 181, 234
18:32 289
23:31-34 181
24:8 183
33:11 289
33:21 137
34:23-24 193
36 137
36:24-27 224
36:33-36 285
37:1-14 .... 137, 186
37:24-25 193
40—48 253
43:4 148

DANIEL
General Info 138, 152
1:1-20 138
2 .... 139, 194
2:44 194
2:47 139
3:1-27 139
3:28-29 139
4:34-37 139
6 139
7 .... 142, 175
                                                  177, 194
7:1-28 153
7:13 139
7:13-14 .... 187, 194
7:15-27 195
8:16 194
9:4-19 149
9:7 149
9:14 149
9:16 149
9:20-24 139
9:21 194
11:2-3 152
11:4 152
12:1-2 .... 186, 222

HOSEA
General Info 126
4:1-3 134
4—10 285
6:6 206
11:1 162

JOEL
3:17-21 285

AMOS
General Info 126
1—6 285
5:21-27 .... 125, 134, 206
9:13-15 285

JONAH
General Info 125
4:2b 125

MICAH
3:9-12 123
6:6-8 206

NAHUM
General Info 126

HABAKKUK
General Info 133
1:5-11 133
2:4 .... 133, 149, 259
2:14 260
3:17-19 133

HAGGAI
General Info 146
2:20-23 145

ZECHARIAH
General Info 148
9:9 178
9:9-17 151
13:1 193
14:9 178

MALACHI
1:6-14 150
2:1-9 150
2:10-15 152
2:16 152
2:17 150
3:1 .... 151, 161
3:5 150
3:6-7 150
3:8-12 150
3:14 150
4:5 .... 151, 161

MATTHEW
1:1 159
1:1-3 162
1:1-17 .... 160, 246
1:18—2:23 160
1:20 160
1:21 246
1:23 2486
2:16 219
3:1a 163
3:1-12 160
3:2 155
3:16-17 161
3:17 163
4:1-11 162
4:5 163
4:17 163
5:10 260
5:17 261
5:20 263
5:20-48 264
5:27 167
5:43-48 .... 167, 263
5—7 165
6:9-13 .... 167, 199

6:14-15 177
6:33 167
8:27 168
9:6 249
9:13 261
10:1-4 167
10:28 .... 213, 268
11:11 177
12:1-6 249
12:1-14 260
12:6 249
12:7 261
13:11-17 165
14:23 252
15:1-20 260
16:13 169
16:14 169
16:15 169
16:16 169
16:20 169
16:21 173
16:22 173
16:24 .... 174, 275
16:25 .... 174, 177
16:28 .... 175, 187
17:1-9 175
17:1-13 219
17:7b 176
17:22-23 176
18:20 246
18:21-35 179
19:1-9 260
19:16-26 177
19:16-30 168
20:17-19 176
20:20-28 177
20:25 167
21:1-11 177
21:4-5 178
21:12-17 .... 178, 267
21:12-22 249
21:13 179
21:23—22:46 179
21:33-44 180
21:45-46 180
22:37-40 261
22:41-46 196
23:1-36 260
23:13-36 261
23:13-18 263
23:23 .... 166, 261
25:31-46 .... 213, 263
26:17-19 211
26:26 181
26:26-29 234
26:27-28 181

MATTHEW (Cont.)

26:38-42	181
26:47-56	182
26:57-68	182
26:60	249
26:64	196
27:1-5	186
27:11-31	184
27:29	196
27:32-56	183
27:37	183, 195
27:40	249
27:46	183, 208
28:18-20	186, 200
28:19	252
28:20	246

MARK

1:1-3	159
1:1-8	163
1:9-11	161
1:11b	161
1:12-13	162
1:15	163
2:7	167, 249
3:1-6	260, 267
3:13-19	167
4:10-12	165
4:41	168
6:46	252
7:1-19	260
8:27	169
8:28	169
8:29a	169
8:29b	169
8:30	169
8:31	173
8:32	173
8:33	174
8:34	174, 275
8:35	177
9:1	175, 187
9:2-10	175
9:2-13	219
9:10	173
9:30-37	176
10:1-12	260
10:17-27	177
10:17-31	168
10:32-34	176
10:35-45	177
10:42	167
10:45	213, 268
10:47-48	160
11:1-10	177
11:12-21	178, 249, 267

11:17	179
11:25	177
11:27—12:40	179
11:28	167
12:1-11	180
12:12	180
12:28-34	261
12:32	254
12:35-37	196
12:38-40	260
14:1-16	211
14:22	181
14:22-25	234
14:24	181
14:34-36	181
14:43-50	182
14:53-65	182
14:57	249
14:62	196
15:1-20	184
15:17	196
15:21-41	183
15:26	183, 195
15:29-30	251
15:34	183, 208

LUKE

1:1	159
1:5	195
1:5-25	194
1:19	194
1:26-27	194
1:27	160
1:30-33	195
1:33b	196
1:35	160
1:39-45	194
1:46-55	195
1:57-80	194
2:1-2	195
2:1-20	160
2:67-79	195
3:1-20	160
3:21-22	161
3:22b	161
4:1-13	162
4:18-19	164, 240
4:21	164
4:22	167
5:21	167
5:24	249
6:1-11	260
6:12	252
6:12-16	167
6:32-38	263
6:37	177

LUKE (Cont.)

7:28	177
7:49	167
8:9-10	165
8:23	174, 275
8:25b	168
9:18	169
9:19	169
9:20a	169
9:20b	169
9:21	169
9:22	173
9:24	177
9:28-36	175, 219
9:31	219
9:43-45	178
9:48	177
9:51	176
9:53	176
10:25-37	263
11:2-4	199
11:37-52	260
11:39-52	263
13:22	176
13:33b	176
15	241
16:19-31	263
17:3	177
17:11	176
18:18-30	168
18:27	177, 213
18:31	176
18:31-34	176
19:1-10	177
19:12-15	200
19:18-27	177
19:27	175, 187
19:28	176
19:28-40	177
19:41	178
19:42-44	178
19:45-48	178, 267
19:46	179
20	179
20:2	167
20:9-18	180
20:19	180
20:41-44	196
22:7-16	211
22:19	181
22:19-20	234
22:20	181
22:42-44	181
22:47-53	182
22:63—23:25	182
22:69	196

23:1-3	195
23:26-49	183
23:34	177
23:38	183, 195
23:43	288
24:27	186
24:44	186
24:48	186
24:51	187, 196

JOHN

1:1	159, 247, 272
1:1-3	244
1:1-5	163
1:4-5	272
1:5	196
1:6-8	160
1:9	272
1:11-13	274
1:14	249
1:15	160
1:18	197, 245, 273
1:19-31	160
1:21	176
1:25	176, 219
1:29	211
1:32-34	161
2:13-25	178, 267
2:19	249
2:21	249
3:16-18	213
3:16-21	273, 287
3:36	273
6:14	176
6:67	167
7:40	176
8:16	286
11:25-26	221, 290
11:50	219
12:12-15	177
12:15	178
12:17	222
12:30-33	273
12:47-48	273
13:1	211
13:1-17	177
13:34-35	264
14:2-3	288
14:5-21	267
15:13	267
15:17	264
15:26	252
16:7	250
16:12-15	252
18:1-14	182
18:14	219

JOHN (Cont.)

18:19-40 182
19:1-16 182
19:2-5 196
19:5 273
19:12-15 198
19:16-37 183
19:19-22 .... 183, 195
21:15-17 186

ACTS

1:1-8 250
1:6 192
1:9 .... 187, 196
1:10 201
1:22 220
2:1-4 250
2:2-12 280
2:23 204
2:24 220
2:24-36 197
2:32 220
2:32-33 252
2:32-39 .... 198, 223
2:36-38 204
2:33 196
2:36b 18
2:42-47 .... 199, 203
3:15 .... 220, 244
3:17-19 223
3:18-19 204
3:22-23 219
4:2 220
4:10-12 204
4:33 220
4:32-35 199
5:30 220
5:30-31 204
6:1-7 201
7:37 219
7:44-50 251
7:55 196
8:26-35 211
10:39-43 204
10:40 220
10:44 286
11:26 230
13:30-37 220
17:7 198
17:18 220
17:22-25 251
17:31 .... 223, 286
17:32 220
23:6-10 220
24:14-16 223
28:31 197

ROMANS

1:18-32 272
1:19-20 244
2:16 286
3:3 241
3:21-26 .... 209, 287
4:3-5 237
4:13-16 287
5:3-5 277
5:6-8 219
5:18-19 .... 213, 289
6:3-4 279
6:10 221
6:15-23 226
7:14—8:4 224
7:7-25 271
8:3-4 .... 264, 286
8:14-17 .... 253, 274, 287
8:17 279
8:18-30 277
8:22-27 255
8:23 290
8:29-30 239
8:34 196
9—11 239
9:1-5 239
9:6 239
9:7-29 239
9:11 239
9:17 239
9:30 239
10:4 264
10:4-12 239
10:9 197
10:4-13 253
11:25-32 .... 213, 289
11:30-32 239
12:1 215
12:1-2 225
13:9-10 201
13:10 264
14:10-12 286
14:11-12 197
15:27 201

I CORINTHIANS

1:22-24 205
2:2 204
3:10-15 288
3:16 251
6:9-10 290
6:18-20 251
7:1-16 266
8:6 .... 197, 252
11:23-26 234
11:26 279

I CORINTHIANS (Cont.)
12:3 197
13 266
15 ....228, 290
15:1-8 186
15:19 222
15:21-22 ....222, 289
15:24-25 202
15:26 202
15:27-38 196
15:36 222
15:49 274
15:54b 196
15:55-57 225
15:58 226

II CORINTHIANS
1:22 274
3:6 240
3:16-18 274
3:18 239
4:4 ....197, 273
4:6-18 276
5:8-10 288
5:10 286
5:14 221
5:17 220
5:17-20 239
5:18-19 214
5:19 ....210, 277
5:21—6:2 240
6:16 251
7:1 225
9:6-15 201
11:18—12:10 277
13:14 252

GALATIANS
2:20 275
3:7 237
3:10-14 213
3:16 238
3:17 60
3:20 252
3:20-21 292
3:26-29 280
3:28 201
4:1-7 225
4:4-7 ....253, 274, 287
4:6 252
5:1-6 236
5:13-14 264
5:14 201
5:16-26 274
5:19-21 290
6:9-10 280

EPHESIANS
1:5 239
1:11 239
1:13 274
1:17 252
1:20 196
2:8-9 236
2:8-10 280
2:10 ....201, 238
2:11-22 238
2:13-22 214
2:15 274
2:19-22 251
4:1 225
4:1-16 254
4:17-19 272
4:20-24 274
4:32 241
5:5 290
5:15-20 251
5:31-32 289
6:5-9 201
6:12 212

PHILIPPIANS
1:27 225
2:3-5 278
2:6-11 278
2:10-11 ....197, 289
2:12-13 224
3:3-4 252
3:10-11 279
3:20a 198
3:20-21 ....198, 290

COLOSSIANS
1:9-10 252
1:12-14 198
1:15 ....197, 273
1:15-20 ....244, 289
1:19-23 214
1:24 276
2:13 241
2:13-15 214
2:15 196
2:17 209
3:1 196
3:1-4 ....198, 225
3:5-10 274
3:11 ....203, 280
3:13 241

I THESSALONIANS
1:2-4 252
1:10 211

308

II THESSALONIANS
1:5-10 223
1:8-10 213

I TIMOTHY
2:1-4 ....213, 289
2:6a 213
4:10...................................213, 222, 289
6:18-19 201

II TIMOTHY
4:1 286

TITUS
2:11..289
3:1..201
3:8..201

PHILEMON
v15-16...203

HEBREWS
General Info....................................206
1:1-3 244
1:3..196, 197, 273
2:9b..221
2:14-15 221
3:4..255
4:15..248
7:22-27 210
8:1..196
9:1-15 210
10:1-2 207
10:3-4 206
10:11-13..210
10:12...196
10:19-22 210
10:19-25 255
10:24-25 ....201, 280
12:2...196
12:24b...209
13:15-16 215

JAMES
1:2-4 277
1:27..201, 215
2:8..264

I PETER
1:2-12 252
2:11-17.......................................254, 280
2:21..274
2:24..213
3:13-17 254
3:20-21 279
3:22..196

4:5..286
4:12-17 254
4:14..277
4:19..280

II PETER
3:5-12 288
3:9..213, 289
3:13..288

I JOHN
1:1..186, 248
2:2..210, 213
2:12..241
3:2-3 290
3:16..267
4:8-11...264
4:12-17 265
4:16..265
4:19..265

REVELATION
5:6-10..196, 211
6:9-11...290
11:15...202
11:18b...211
13...212
14:9-12 213
17—19...212
18:21-24 200
19:6-9 289
20:11-15.............................213, 223, 288
21:1-4 ....198, 202, 289
21:3...253
21:7-8 ....200, 290
21:22...253
21—22...286
22:5...291
22:20-21 293

Made in the USA
Columbia, SC
02 July 2019